Chapter 1

It was one of those days when I just felt like sitting on the settee watching television. The weather was blowing a gale, rain rattled against the windowpanes and draughts sneaked under the door, making me wish summer would arrive.

My mind was beginning to wander, and I turned my head to look out of the window, watching the raindrops as they ran down the windowpane. I sighed, wishing something exciting would happen, when a voice from the television attracted my attention to a voice reading the offer below.

"Are you looking for an unusual one-time only experience? This experience is being offered with a monetary payment to the right person. To enter this competition, send a postcard with your name and address, adding the reason you feel you should win to the address below. (Address was added) All entries must reach this office before the last day of April. Any entries received after this date will be discounted.

I quickly grabbed a pen and paper and wrote down the details. 'Nothing ventured, nothing gained.' I thought.

I had two weeks before my entry had to be in, so I had time to come up with a good reason why I should win. Easier said than done. I went from not having a holiday for many years to I am grieving the loss of my guinea pig and everything in between.

At the end of the first week, I knew I had to get my entry in the post, so with fingers crossed I wrote:

'I deserve to win this is experience.'

Because I'm living by myself

I might get the chance to meet a man.

Who will take me off the shelf?

I stuck a first-class stamp on the postcard and popped it into the local Post Office to be sure it was sent.

The following week dragged by, I did all the usual things, housework, shopping, catching up with friends on the internet. I also went through my closet and tried on my clothes to see which ones were suitable for 'an unusual experience.'. (Ever the optimist me.)

A couple of days later there was a knock on my door. 'Who can that be?' I asked myself. I patted my hair and rushed to answer it. Through the glass in my front door, I could see the outline of two people, a man who was rather short and a woman who was exceedingly tall. I cautiously opened the door and asked if I could help them. 'Good morning,' the man asked, 'are you Miss Fanny Fernickety?' I looked between the two of them, which was more up and down than left to right, then replied 'Yes that's me.'

'I am – Wing Commander Johnny Kamikarzi and this is my colleague, Wing Commander Betty Bouncers.' Being the polite person I am, I replied, 'How do you do, how may I help you?' 'It is to do with the competition for an unusual experience you entered few weeks ago, The Experience of a Lifetime. We chose ten entries that impressed us, one of which was yours, and put them into hat. Well, it was a beer glass that somehow found its way back to our office after a liquid lunch. However, I digress. Your name was the first one that came out, so here we are.' As you can imagine, I was rather shocked, but I opened the door wider and invited them in.

Wing Commander Kamikarzi took off his hat and handed it to me, as did Wing Commander Bouncers, which I placed on the top of the bookcase in my hall. I led them into the kitchen and offered them a drink. 'Tea, Coffee?' I asked. Wing Commander Kamikarzi asked for a coffee, sitting watching me. Wing Commander Bouncers asked for water and glanced around the room. I offered them a biscuit which they declined, so I sat down at the table.

'Right,' said Wing Commander Kamikarzi 'let me tell you all about the experience and what it will entail. This is unusual, as you will be flying high in way.' 'Oh' I exclaimed, 'I did feel it would be something different. Can you please tell me more about it?'

Wing Commander Kamikarzi looked towards Wing Commander Bouncers with an enquiring look on his face. She then took over the conversation. 'Miss Fernickety, as you must have realised, we are from the British Airforce, and we are looking for a female member of the public to take part in an experiment of a sort. In the first instant you will be asked to come with us to Base Benevolant where we will carry out a series of tests. If you pass these, you will be given more information about the .... umm .... full experience.

We have taken rooms in the pub down the road and will give you a couple of days to think about our offer. You can come and see us any time if you have any questions or wish clarification.

You will need to pack enough clothes for a week only, as you will be issued with special clothing if you pass the tests and if you accept our offer.' Should you fail, you will be paid a sum of one thousand pounds rising to two thousand pounds should you pass. If you decidnot to take part, you will only receive five hundred pounds. Obviously, we hope you will agree, especially now we have seen you.

I sat there sipping my tea with all sorts of chaotic thoughts going through my mind.

They finished their drinks and rose to their feet. 'We will leave you now, but don't forget we are just down the road if you need us.' I nodded and showed them to the door. They collected their hats and saying their goodbyes walked through the door and left. I stood in the doorway and watched the odd couple walk down the road towards the The Right Royal Ruckas Pub. When they disappeared inside the pub I stepped back and closed my door.

Chapter 2

I had so much to think about. Five hundred pounds would look good in my bank account, but two thousand would look even better. I decided to sleep on it. I washed up the mugs and the glass and put them away. Putting on my coat, I went for a walk along the riverbank to clear my head.

I met up with a neighbour of mine, Mrs Una Unfortunate with her dog, Fluffy Wuffy. 'Good afternoon,' I called, 'how are you today?' I knew it was a mistake directly the words came out of my mouth. While I fussed Fluffy Wuffy, who was carrying a stick in his mouth that he kept hitting me with. This was causing me to do a hoppity sort of dance to try to avoid it. Mrs Unfortunate proceeded to tell me about all her aches and pains. I am surprised the woman is still able to walk! She is riddled with arthritis from head to toe, has sinus trouble, is deaf in one ear, doesn't sleep well and to top it all, has found out she is allergic to peanuts. There I was, nodding my head while trying to avoid a beating and desperately trying to escape this form of torture.

Luckily a friend of mine, Ginny Vagaries walked up behind me. 'Hi Fanny, I'm so glad I've caught you.' she said. 'Are you going my way? If so, we can chat on the way.' I had never been so pleased to see anyone in my life and agreed to walk with her. Saying goodbye to Mrs Unfortunate, we headed off in the opposite direction. 'Oh Ginny, I am so grateful to you. I thought I would never get away from that woman, and as for her dog, I will have bruises all over my legs come tomorrow.' Chuckling, we walked on together generally chatting about this and that. Then I had a sudden thought.

'Ginny,' I asked, 'if I were to go away for a week or two, would you be kind enough to keep an eye on my house for me and Tigerfeet? I would give you a key if you wouldn't mind, perhaps you would also water my plants for me.' Ginny said she would be more than happy to do that.

We eventually came to a split in the path. A signpost indicated that the path to the left went to Lower Threadbare and the right, Upper Threadbare. Ginny was going to visit her Aunt Peculiar in Lower Threadbare where she had a cottage at the end of Blanketstitch Lane. As I looked at her in askance at the name Aunt Peculiar she laughed and told me her Aunty was really called Petunia, but she had some strange habits. For example, when there is a full moon, she goes out into the garden at midnight and sings to the faery folk. This upsets her neighbour as she has an awful voice and sings as loudly as she can. We chuckled over this, and Ginny told me there was worse than that. She is a very large lady and her garden backs onto the Church car park. Her washing line is at the bottom of her garden, and she takes great delight in hanging a week's worth of her very large bloomers, hanging them out Sundays in time for the morning service. If there is a gentle breeze, they just flutter gently to and fro, but if there is a gale force wind, they fill up like barrage balloons. Said bloomers are old fashioned and are an awful shade of faded red which draws the eye, to the consternation of the congregation, especially the men.

(*Ginny was a superb teller of tales and by this time, we were both almost bent double with laughter*) 'And.' She added, 'what makes it worse was that a gang of teenagers have taken to hanging about together in the car park when people were arriving for church and chanting

"Look at those bloomers, they'd make good tents, which would house fifty gents!"

And other equally silly rhymes. Vicar Mucinous McPious and various other members of the congregation have asked Aunt to please not hang them out on a Sunday or at least move her clothesline back closer to the house. Aunt informed everyone that her late husband (very late!) had put that clothesline in soon after they were married and moved into this house and there no way she would allow it to be moved. She had worked very hard on her garden, and she had it just how she liked it being easily to maintain. She also added that her faeries would be very upset as they lived among the flowers.

Ginny then suggested we sit on a nearby seat while she tells me the rest of the story. 'Vicar McPious had brought this situation on himself. He lived in the Manse next to the church and he had called the Police when he could no longer stand the noise she made singing to the faeries. There she was, happily singing away when she heard sirens which were coming closer and closer. There was a screeching of brakes and two Policemen burst through her side gate and into her back garden. Looking around they began to look puzzled. 'Hello Danny Dusslittle and Bart Bejavers' Aunty called, 'whatever are you doing here? I haven't seen you two boys since you climbed the steeple of the church and hung a skull and crossbones flag at the top. They all laughed together recalling how long it had taken to remove it and how lucky they were not to have been caught or they wouldn't have been accepted into the Police Force. 'So,' Aunty repeated, 'why are you here?' Bart took over saying they had received a phone call saying it sounded like someone was being murdered in your garden. When Aunty enquired who had phoned, they told her in confidence that it was the old fart of a Vicar McPious. At that Aunty began to laugh, saying that war had now been declared. She quickly went indoors and returned clutching a very aged megaphone. 'Murder is being done, is it?' she muttered, 'I'll give him murder, the sanctimonious pig-faced fat putrid-arsed prig' With that, she held the megaphone to her lips and began ummm – her form of singing again. It was so loud it could be heard far and wide, to many different reactions from the residents. Danny and Bart allowed her to continue for a few minutes and then firmly confiscated the megaphone. Giving Aunty a quick hug they headed back to the office to put in a report. They then wickedly phoned the Vicar to tell him it was only Aunty singing to the faeries and there wasn't much they could do about it because he was the only one who had complained. Besides, it was only once a month or so. The Vicar then complained it had got very, very loud and was informed that would not happen again, without telling him they had confiscated a megaphone.

Meanwhile Aunty had said goodnight to the faeries, smiling to herself as she heard the Vicar's cats serenading the female cats in the area. As she went indoors, she heard the Vicar's bedroom window open and heard him shouting out 'Samson, stop that infernal row this minute or I will empty the contents of this gozunder over your bloody head.'

I asked Ginny if she would take me to meet her Aunty sometime as I felt there were many more stories about her. One day perhaps I will write a book about her, she needs to go down in history. However, standing up I gave Ginny a hug and promised to let her know if I decided to go on holiday.

Chapter 3

Walking quickly back I decided I would take the trial and went straight to the Right Royal Ruckas Pub and let the Wing Commanders know. When I reached the Pub, they were sitting in the beer garden watching a game of Boules. When Wing Commander Kamikarzi caught sight of me, he immediately rose to his feet and pulled out a chair for me to sit down. He offered me a drink and I asked what Wing Commander Bouncer was drinking. It's a local wine, Blanc Deville, I was told and agreed to have one of those. Wing Commander Kamikarzi emptied his glass in one swallow and went to the bar to order the drinks. While he was gone, I asked Wing Commander Bouncers how she was enjoying country life. 'Well,' she replied, 'we've not been here long but I must say I feel really relaxed.' 'Probably due to the wine.' I thought to myself. When Wing Commander Kamikarzi returned, he was carrying my wine and a beer he said was called Wickedly-Wilde Ale. I asked him if he had any painkillers with him because I felt he would need them come morning. We sat for a while sipping our drinks and generally chatting. I began to feel very relaxed and decided it was time I told them of my decision.

'So,' I said, 'I have been giving a lot of thought to your offer and have decided to accept it. Where do we go from here?' Wing Commander Kamikarzi told me he was delighted, as was Wing Commander Bouncers. They told me they would come to my house in the morning and bring all the paperwork, etc, with them. I shook their hands and wandered very carefully home. 'That was some wine.' I thought.

By the time I got indoors it was well past dinner time, so I grabbed a ready meal out of the freezer and pinged it in the microwave. While I was waiting for my meal to cook, I took a couple of painkillers cos I knew I would wake up with a headache in the morning otherwise. I grabbed a knife and fork, a piece of kitchen roll and a plate and set them on the table. When the meal was ready, I tipped it onto my plate and sat down to eat. 'What have I done?' I asked myself, 'I do hope I haven't made the biggest mistake of my life.' I picked up Sunday's paper and checked out my horoscope.

"This is a week for making decisions.' I read, *'Opportunities could come your way which will take you out of your comfort zone, but if you are brave enough, it is time to take a chance."*

'Well, that has told me,' I thought, 'I am going adventuring.

I decided to phone Ginny and tell her I was going to take the holiday, but if still ok with her I would leave a key under the flowerpot by my front door.   I quickly did the washing up, put the plate and utensils away and decided to get my suitcase out of the cupboard under the stairs. As is usual, it was right at the back, so I had to start removing everything else in there. What I thought was going to be a five-minute job took much longer. Inside I found two tennis rackets, one of which needed restringing, a golf club that used to belong to my Dad, a guitar from my pro hippy days that I bought on a whim thinking I would be able to learn to play it, two bags of plastic bags, an old sewing machine, on which I was going to make my own patchwork quilt – of course, that never came to fruition either. Having placed that outside, there was still more to get through. The next items were a personal file full of papers, which I thought I had better look through later, followed by a box of Christmas decorations, a small artificial Christmas tree, another cardboard box full of what I can only call bric-a-brac. Just a couple more things and I would be able to grab the suitcase. Not much more left. One small suitcase, which, when opened, contained craft stuff from the time I had a craze for card making. Finally, A large supermarket bag containing handbags I no longer use. (I know, what the hell was I doing hanging onto all this stuff - my excuse – they might come in handy, or I might want to take up crafting again.)

Chapter 4

Having grabbed my suitcase, I put everything else back in, except for the personal file which I put on the kitchen table. The suitcase was rather dusty, so I wheeled that the kitchen too. With trepidation I open the case and breathed a sigh of relief to find it was empty. I quickly dusted it and then gave it a quick wipe with a household cleaner. I didn't go and sort out what I was going to pack because I didn't know what the weather would be like where I was going, if I passed the test that is. I waited to ask the Wing Commanders when they came to visit in the morning.

I made myself a cup of tea, found a chocolate cupcake and sat down at the table to go through the personal file. I realised this had belonged to my parents and I had put it away after they passed because I couldn't face going through it. Feeling rather excited, because I had no idea what was in there, I unclipped the fastening and lifted the lid. It was a concertina type of file which feel open exposing papers and black and white photos inside. 'Ok,' I said to myself, 'I'll start at A and work through.

A - This held nothing to do with the letter A at all. In fact, it held nothing of interest apart from a letter from a relative who lived in Canada. I took the letter out of the envelope and saw it was from Great Aunt Agnes. (Hence in A) I read the letter through, they had had very bad snowstorms. The roof fell in on the cattle shed. Bertie Bombastica, whoever he was, had come to help fix it. Bertie had fallen in love with her daughter, Annalina Felicitas, and they had run away together. They had also run off with the silver and the household cash box. She had said she would let my parents know the outcome,

Unfortunately, there was no follow up letter in

B – Banks – This contained details of bank and a <u>couple</u> of new old cheque books.

C – A map of Chester and a guidebook were inside here. As well as a couple of black and white photos of my parents outside Chester Cathedral. This brought tears to my eyes as I studied their lovely smiling faces. I also found some old Christmas cards, one of which was to them from me.

D – An old diary which I flicked through briefly and decided to keep it out to read through properly later.

E – Electricity Bills. Elastic bands, perished.

F - Agenda for trip to France including the Eiffel Tower. Photos of my parents in front of it, some old French Francs, and some odd coins.

G – Old packets of garden seeds and equally old gardening magazines. A Pamphlet on the use of a gas mask. (I did wonder where the gas mask was as I would have loved to have it because I understand it blew raspberry sounds when worn.)

H – A list of Household expenses in £ s d.

Strangely, there was also a gentleman's handkerchief with the initials HH embroidered on it in one corner. (I wondered who HH was, another thing to investigate in the future.)

I – This had a spare index in it and instructions on how to grow Gourds plus the seeds. (I did wonder whether they would still grow.)

J – A pencil drawing entitled Jiggery Pokery by Artie Krayon. (J was empty apart from that.)

K – Instructions and Diagram on how to build a box kite. A pamphlet entitled Kingdom Come which had words crossed out and new ones inserted. (I do feel it should now be entitled Kingdom Doesn't Come.)

L – Land Registry details on a house they sold ten years before they passed. There were also loose Lexicon cards, which brought back happy memories of when we all play the game together.

M – Instructions on how to play a mouth organ and mouth organ tunes for beginners.

N – A New World map. Manuscripts for marching tunes and, most necessary, instructions on how to make your own indoor air raid shelter. I was tempted to put the manuscripts in the M folder and, after debating where the air raid shelter instructions should go, A or I, decided to leave them where they were.

O – An Old Testament book with Mum's name written in it and a copy of the Owl and The Pussy Cat.

P – Paper cuttings of their wedding announcement. Pattern for a wedding dress, which I assume was Mums. A packet of paper chains. Photos of people I don't know, although there were names on the back – Mary and Fred at the Hippodrome, Little Molly ready for school, Hastings Pier, Hilda horse riding (Hilda looked more like a horse than the horse.) And Leeds Castle, which, unfortunately could only vaguely be seen as it was foggy.

Q – Nothing here except dust and a hair grip.

R – Receipts, rather a lot of them, but one made me smile because it was for a bag of broken biscuits.

S – Invitations to the Skuttlebutt Ball. Savings books with a zero balance.

T – Testimonials.　Old toothpaste coupon 5d off. A garden tool catalogue. Packet of Tracing paper.

U/V – Underwear catalogue. Victory leaflet. Booklet on Victorian inventions.

W – Work Rotas. Receipt for a Stone water bottle.

X/Y – Yesteryear remembered in Song programme. Yodelling made easy instructions.

Z – Zinc Bath catalogue. Scribbled notes about zeppelins with sketches.

Apart from trying to work out the hanky with the HH initials embroidered on it and the old diary, there wasn't much more of interest, so I closed the file and returned it to the cupboard. I put the hanky and the diary on a shelf in the kitchen and, as time was getting on, I decided to head off to bed. I thought I would lay awake for hours, but unusually promptly fell asleep.

Chapter 5

The following day I awoke to the sound of birdsong and checking the time I was surprised to see it was already 8.30am. Trying to clear my mind, I struggled out of bed. 'That really was some wine I imbibed last night.' I thought to myself. I headed towards the bathroom, had a quick wee, took a shower, cleaned my teeth and, feeling more human, went back to my bedroom to get dressed. I decided to wear jeans and a jumper as I was unsure what the itinerary was likely to be.

As I didn't know what time the Wing Commanders would arrive, I had a piece of toast and marmite and a cup of tea for breakfast. After doing the washing up, I headed back upstairs to go through my clothes again, which I sorted into piles. Winter and Summer. I returned any I felt unsuitable back into the wardrobe, leaving two smallish piles on the bed. I grabbed a weeks' worth of underwear, socks, etc, which I put in a separate pile. I also added the diary and the hanky embroidered with HH as I was sure I would have time to spare while away.

I headed back downstairs just as a loud knocking came at the front door. 'This must be them.' I thought heading towards the door. As I opened it, I heard a groaning noise and there in the doorway stood two very sorry looking Wing Commanders. Wing Commander Kamikarzi had a black eye and a swollen lip, while Wing Commander Bouncers was wearing a pair of crooked glasses, held together with a band aid plaster. (I cannot tell a lie I felt a smirk cross my face.) 'Good morning,' I said, 'do come in.'

I led them towards the kitchen and suggested they take a seat at the table. I put the kettle on in readiness of making them both a black coffee. As they sat down, they groaned in unison. 'Umm, exciting night then at the Right Royal Ruckas?' I asked, 'It's living up to its name then?' They nodded in reply. I turned to make them a black coffee, which I placed before them before I sat down. 'What happened then?' I enquired.

Wing Commander Kamukarzy spoke first. 'After you left last night, a live group called 'Nigel and The Rocking Knockers' or something similar, began to play some Rock n Roll music. We were sitting at our table minding our own business when this rather gobby farmer looking bloke came towards us and grabbed hold of Betty's arm, wanting her to dance with him. Betty declined his offer, and he started shouting abuse at her. Obviously, I asked him to leave her alone and he suddenly swung at me, knocking me to the floor. While I was down on the floor I grabbed him around the ankles, pulling him over. He fell with a rather loud crash and we spent the next few minutes rolling over and over while punching each other. Eventually I grabbed him by his ears and banged his head on the floor, but he caught me with an uppercut catching me below the chin, causing me to bite my lip. By now we were surrounded by a mob of drunken yobs yelling suggestions such as 'knee him in the groin, bite his ear off, poke yer fingers up 'is nose and other equally salubrious suggestions.'

At this point, Betty took up the story. 'It was a very one-sided fight, so I grabbed a couple of empty wine bottles from behind the bar and broke them over a couple of the blokes' heads. I started to kick and push the men out of the way and blew the whistle I always carry with me ready for problems like this. We never go anywhere without a back-up and four of our large airmen entered the room laying about the crowd with cudgels. In the affray my glasses got knocked off, but luckily the lenses remained intact.

Unfortunately, we have been asked to vacate the premises and have had to pay for any breakages.

You have no idea how hard it was to keep a straight face, but then I saw Betty's shoulders begin to shake. 'Oh my,' she stuttered, 'I haven't enjoyed myself so much in years. I just hope that word of it doesn't get back to headquarters or we could both be in deep do-doos! And please call us Betty and Johnny when we are off duty.' Johnny also began to laugh, shouting, 'Stop it, my lip hurts.'

And there we were, all three of us in fits of giggles. 'Where are the fellows with the cudgels?' I asked. 'They are outside waiting in the back of the truck. We are going to make a quick getaway, so please can you grab what you want to bring with you, and we will be off. We will head straight back to our HQ and take it from there.' 'Nothing ventured, nothing gained.' I reminded myself, rushing upstairs to throw my clothes into my wheely suitcase, plus the diary and HH hanky, makeup, toothbrush and, grabbing my handbag, purse, mobile phone, and bank cards, I headed straight back downstairs. I had placed a spare key under the flowerpot for Ginny before I went to bed last night. I checked my backdoor was locked, grabbed my door keys, and headed towards the front door behind Betty and Johnny. Betty was wheeling my suitcase and Johnny took my keys and locked the door behind us. I found myself being lifted into the front of the truck, while my suitcase was passed up into the back.

And we were off..............

Chapter 6

The Secret Airbase

Code Name Blue November

And so it begins

Wing Commander Kamikarzi , sorry Johnny, was doing the driving and he didn't hang about. I was sitting between him and Betty in the front of the truck. Betty and I chatted about general things learning more about each other. Betty surprised me by telling me she writes books like those published by Mills & Boon. The plot of her latest book is unbelievable. It is to be called the Final Docking and was about an astronaut who had fallen in love with an alien from another planet. She had named him Astrotom and she was called Aphidrosa. I looked at her in askance at their names, but she nodded, saying, 'Yes, that's really what I have called them.' She laughed adding, 'as long as they sell, they don't look too closely at the plot or the names.'

We stopped for lunch at an out of the way pub known as Lost in Ignominy. Johnny had called ahead and ordered trays of sandwiches and sausage rolls to be waiting for us. We were taken to a private room and were given half an hour to eat and make ourselves comfortable before we continued onwards.

Betty poured teas and coffees and passed them round. She then came and sat beside me at the table. She told me we should reach HQ by six o'clock this evening. After we arrive you will be taken to a facility on site. It is basic, but everything you need will be provided. She suggested I just relax and in the morning the tests will begin.

My accommodation was indeed basic but had everything I needed. It was a large bedroom with an ensuite. Not only was there a king-sized bed, but also a settee and matching armchair arranged so I could watch the television or enjoy the view out of the window. I stood for a while at the window enjoying said view, fields of swaying grasses, woods behind and hills in the distance. I decided if I had the opportunity, I would like to take a walk through those fields to the woods. Turning back, I noticed a shelf with several books on it, as well as an A LaCarte menu, with a note attached telling me to feel free to order whatever I would like, and it would be brought to me. The books were of more interest, a Bible, Crossword puzzles, two of Bettys books, which made me smile, and finally, a copy of The Hitchhikers Guide to the Galaxy. I wondered how many others had spent time here and taken the 'tests. 'I'm sure I will find out tomorrow.' I told myself.

Picking up the menu, I sat down to read through it. There was a great deal of choice.

Menu

Starters

Soup of the Day, served with a bread roll and butter.

Stuffed Mushrooms served with hot toasted garlic bread triangles.

Chicken Gorgons served with a dip of your choice – bbq, mild chilli, garlic mayo, or our own Tomato Sauce.

Mains

Roast Beef/Chicken/Lamb - with all the trimmings - Roast Potatoes and Parsnip, Swede and Carrot Mash,

Seasonal Vegetables, Yorkshire Pudding, various sauces, and Chef's Special Gravy.

Gammon with Egg & Pineapple served with Thick Thrice Cooked Chips or New Potatoes.

Country Farmer's Chicken and Bacon Pie, served with Onion Mash and Chef's Special Gravy.

Porkies Pork Sausages, Mash and Onion Rings (gravy optional.)

Sweets

Knickerbocker Glory

Banana Split with caramel fudge sauce and ice-cream.

Crème Brule

Salted Caramel Apple Hetty served with English Custard/Ice Cream/Spray Cream

Lemon or Chocolate Torte served with Cream or Ice-cream

Jam RolyPoly served with English Custard

Treacle Suet Pudding (like Grandma used to make) served with English Custard

Light Bites

Cheesy Chips

Sandwiches – Cheese n Pickle

Ham Salad

Chicken n sage & onion stuffing

Egg n Cress

Pizzas -

Three Cheese

Peperami

Hawaian

Picking up the phone, I decided to ask what the soup of the day was. It was Leek & Potato, one of my favourites, so I ordered this and a roll. Within minutes there was a knock at my door and there stood a very arresting young man. He was tall, with blond hair and brown eyes. He had an earring in one ear and his smile was attractively crooked. (Yes, that thought did cross my mind. However, it soon left when he opened his mouth.) His identity card said he was Tim Bucktoo.

"Hello Mith, here ith your thoup and roll. When you have finithed it, pleathe jutht plathe the tray outhide your door and I will make thure it ith collected later. Ith there anything elthe I can do for you? (Yeth, I thought, you can wipe the thpit off my face!)

'No thank you', I replied, 'you have done more than enough for me. I bid you goodnight.'

I must admit the thoup was delicious. It was just enough to fill the hole in my tummy. As instructed, I left the tray and dishes outside the door. Made sure the door was locked, and decided to go to bed early as I was feeling rather weary. I had a quick wash and changed into my jammies, climbed into bed, and promptly fell asleep.

Chapter 7

Test Day at last

I was woken up by a ringing in my ears. Somehow, I became confused and incorporated the ringing into my dream. I was standing at the top of a church steeple with a skull and crossbow flag in my hands. I was surrounded by miniature policemen who were chanting 'Eei eei eei oh, up the flagpole it must go, if you fail, we'll push you over and you will not land in clover.'

Suddenly the ringing started to invade my mind and I jumped awake. Grabbing the phone I mumbled, 'Hello.' 'Good morning,' said Betty, 'time to rise and shine.' I will come by in about an hour and take you to the Naafi for breakfast. Over breakfast we will reveal the tests you will be taking today. You will then be provided with any equipment you need. See you soon. Bye for now.'

I lay still in bed for a moment. 'Oh My,' I thought, test day is here.' I could feel the excitement rising in me. I sorted out the clothes I would wear. A pair of smart trousers and a woollen tabard type top. Clean underwear of course. I went into the bathroom and took a shower, washed my hair, and cleaned my teeth. Back into the bedroom to get dressed, and quickly blow-dry my hair. I repacked my suitcase as I was unsure where I would be spending the next day or so.

I put on a bit of makeup and gathered the bits and pieces I would need to take with me. The hour must have flown by, because I was just about to go and unlock the door, when there was a knock and Betty called, 'Helloooo. It's me.'

And Betty stood there in all her glory wearing her smart uniform. 'Come,' she said, 'lots to get through today. You can leave your stuff here because you will be coming back this evening.' I smiled at her and thanked her, locked the door, and shoved the key into my small shoulder bag. On the way to breakfast Betty explained I must address her a Ma'am and Johnny as Sir while I am being put through my paces and tests. I told her I fully understood the reason for this and told her I couldn't wait to start what will probably be the most exciting day of my life.

We opted for a Full English breakfast that would see us through the day. I told her about my waiter last night who delivered my Thoup, and laughing she said she had had the same reaction. She did agree he was very handsome but told me there was a waiter who would have been more difficult to cope with. Apparently, the poor man has a stutter, and soup is a very difficult word for him. 'Oh my.' She added, 'he is on duty this morning. Prepare yourself and don't you dare look at me when he repeats our order.'

'G g g g g good m m m morning, m m may I t t t take y y y your or or or order?

Betty asked for the Full English breakfast, with scrambled egg instead of fried. Toast and butter too please.

I concentrated on the menu, and without lifting my head, I mumbled, 'I would like the Full English breakfast, but without the mushrooms or fried tomato, and I would like my egg to be hard fried please. I would also like toast and butter.

We both then sat holding our breaths as we watched him lick the lead in his pencil let said pencil hover over notepad and repeated as he wrote –

'F f f full Eng eng eng English b b b breakfast, s s s scrambled e e e egg, n n n not f f f fried. T t t toast a a a and b b b butter. T t t tea o o o or c c c Coffee?'

'Tea please.' Betty replied.

Then it was my order: 'A a a as a a a above, w w w with h h h hard f f f fried e e e egg. H h h hold t t t the m m m mushrooms and t t t tomato. T t t toast a a a and b b b butter'. (*I couldn't stand it anymore*) Tea please I shouted. 'T t t tea.' He confirmed.

He smiled at us both and walked away to place our orders.

Picking up my serviette, I stuffed it in my mouth as I looked into Betty's eyes. My eyes were watering, and so were hers. When the waiter had gone through the door into the kitchen, we allowed a snort of laughter to escape. We did manage to control ourselves and at last Betty went into the details of the Tests I would be taking that day and what they would involve.

The waiter returned with our breakfasts, which he placed in front of us and then went back to collect our tea. Luckily, he saw we were talking, so didn't interrupt us.

I could not believe what I was going to be doing. I was to be fitted with a full body suit with electrodes that will be sending information to a set of computers that will be recording my body's reactions. There were to be at least three tests, but I had to pass one to move onto the next.

Having finished eating, 'Betty said, Ok, let's go get you fitted for the suit.' 'Yes Ma'am!' I replied. We both rose to our feet, I grabbed my bag, and, like Elvis, we left the building.

A black car was waiting for us outside. A uniformed man got out of the car and walked round to open the back door nearest the pavement. Betty climbed in first and I followed her. The door was closed, and the driver got back in behind the wheel. 'This car is bullet proofed,' said Betty, and we are going to a secret facility. Hence the outriders who will be surrounding us until we get there.

I was beginning to feel extremely nervous now. 'What have I let myself in for?' I asked myself. Betty patted me on the arm and told me to relax, everything will be fine.

After a while I could see a building in the distance surrounded by a high fence. Betty told me it was an electric fence and was guarded day and night. We were driven to a gate. A sentry came to the car and asked for identification. Betty showed her pass, and the gate was opened and in we drove.

'Here we are,' Betty said, 'let the fun begin!'

Chapter 8

The Fun Beginithed

I was led into a locker room inside the building. I glanced around and turned to Betty. 'Ok, what's next?'

Betty told me she was going to help me into the special suit I would need to wear during the tests. She led me towards a cubicle and pulled back the curtain. Inside there was a strange bodysuit, a cream coloured all in one with a zip fastening up the front. The electrodes had wires leading from them that ran to plug type things on the sides. Betty left me to get undressed and asked me to call her if I needed help. It was quite difficult donning the suit. I sat down and started by pulling it over my feet, up my legs to my waist, it wasn't too hard putting my arms in, but I had to call Betty in to help me as I couldn't lift it up onto my shoulders nor do the zip up as I had mittens covering my fingers and hands. Betty soon dealt with fitting me in it and zipping it up.

She went into another cubicle, which had a locked door, took out a key and unlocked and opened it. What she brought out was like leather pieces of armour. I stood there while she Started to place them over the bodysuit. I could hear clicking sounds, and she told me it was the electrodes being clicked into performinators.

'Ready?' she asked. I nodded and I creaked my way out of the changing room and down a hall into a large room with monitors around the walls,and wires everywhere in trunking, for the various pieces of equipment, which made no sense to me whatsoever.

There was a humming from the monitors and standing behind them were people in white coats (scientists I guessed) and headphones. Suddenly an overhead light turned on and highlighted a piece of machinery.

Johnny stepped from behind one of the monitors and came forward to meet me. 'This is the first test, please come this way.' 'Yes Sir.' I replied and followed him towards the piece of equipment. Johnny explained what would happen, and asked if I was still happy to go ahead. He and Betty had both been tested on the machines and had, of course, passed. The test would only take five minutes to complete. I would then be taken to a rest room while my test results would be reviewed. I agreed to take part, wondering if I would regret it.

Johnny pointed out two feet shapes that were in the middle of a large metal hoop. I stepped onto the foot pads and Johnny bent down to fix clasps that would hold my feet in place. Hanging from above, were two hand holds, also made of metal and with clasps, and when locked held my arms up in a V shape. These clasps were clicked and then wires were fitted to my suit from around the hoop. Checking I felt comfortable, Johhny stepped back and returned to stand behind the monitors.

Even though I knew what was about to happen, I did feel a bit apprehensive. A whirring sound heralded the start of the test. The hoop started to spin round and round, getting faster and faster. I felt myself lose consciousness then returning to consciousness, feeling the hoop begin to slow down gradually to a halt.

Johnny was heading towards me, checking I was ok. He asked how I felt and undid the clasps on my hands and feet. When he was sure I was steady enough, he took my hand an helped me down to the ground. I was surprised to find I didn't seem to have any ill effects from the test. Betty came forward next and led me to a sunny room with a couch and a table with flasks of hot water to enable me to make a drink of tea or coffee. There was also bottled water and a plate of finger food. Which waiter brought these I wondered. I made myself a cup of tea and ate an egg and cress sandwich and a sausage roll.

Meanwhile, the scientists were comparing the results from the monitors. They had printed off sheets from their separate monitors and were standing around a table making even more notes.

After further discussion a result was registered on a paper on a clipboard that had my name on the top and details of the tests in the order they would be taken. There was also a column where results were awarded.

It would seem I passed the first test, as Betty came back to let me know I was proceeding to the next test.

This test was totally different. Johnny explained what to expect and assured me it was safe. I was laid on my tummy on a couch type thing and once again plugged in and secured with straps holding me in place. I was also fitted with a crash helmet. Looking forward I could see rails that disappeared into darkness beyond.

A minute or so later, a horn sounded, and I was basted forward at a rate of knots, or should that be miles per hour or even the speed of light? I was halted and brought backwards to the start position. I cannot tell a lie, this test brought tears to my eyes, I dribbled and peed a little. Johnny once again came forward to help me out of the contraption, removed the crash helmet and helped me to my feet. 'I am pleased to say you have passed this test too. Your heartbeat is very strong and regular, and you didn't pass out at all. Well done. Betty will take you to the rest room again. I strongly suggest you try to take a nap; you have two hours until the last test today. Well done.'

Betty came and led me to the changing room once more, saying, 'You don't need to wear this outfit for the last test, so I suggest you change back to your normal clothes. You will be more comfortable in them.' She stayed to help me remove the armour bits first, after unplugging the electrodes and then unzipped the bodysuit and helped me free myself from the gloves and sleeves. She left me to remove the rest and put my own clothes back on. I certainly felt more comfortable to be sure.

Back at the rest room I noticed a pillow and a throw on the settee. As I was feeling rather weary, I decided to take Johnny's advice. Betty told me she would come and wake me in a couple of hours and left, closing the door behind her.

I did fall asleep, but had the strangest thing happen. I could feel something poking me, it was quite painful and opened my eyes to see an Alien being standing before me. It kept poking me with a very long finger. It then started to talk in a language I had not heard before. 'Getum upsy – ooaugh owers. 'What?' I shouted as the fickle finger of fate poked me again. 'Getum upsy!' Poke poke poke. 'Ok,' I replied, 'I am getum upsying.'

Then Betty appeared, she had turned into a lamp post and had a flashing light on her head, I blinked and saw she was also dressed as a policeman. 'Ello, ello, ello – wots goin on here?' she asked. And then turned on her eeeaww eeeaww loudspeaker. The Alien turned to poke her and at the same time I was getum upsying.

Meanwhile the fickle finger of fate that had been continually poking each of us fell off. It was now a phantom fickle finger of fate. Alien started to cry, 'Minepokeron, minepokeron.' Without any further thought, Betty grabbed his pokeron and proceeded to poke the alien. Then, as quick as a flash, Betty snapped his pokeron in half and shoved the bits up his nose holes. From my getum upsying position I reached up and turned off the stupid flashing light and grabbed her eeeaww eeeaww loudspeaker and threw it across the room. It took exception at this treatment and after a final eeeeee, died.

Alien continued to cry, and I noticed he had green blood looking stuff pouring from his missing finger hole, being as quick thinking as I am, I grabbed a leftover egg and cress sandwich and stuffed it in the missing finger hole.

Betty began stamping her feet and demanding the return of her eeeaaww.

Chapter 9

There was a knocking at the door. Waking up I looked around the room. No Alien, no lamp post dressed as a policeman with flashing light – it was only a dream or even more, a nightmare.

'Come in.' I called.

'I hope you managed to get a nap.' Betty said, adding, your last test today doesn't need you to change your clothes, although you will be fitted with special boots.' 'What are they like?' I asked and was told they are a bit like old fashioned diver's boots and are rather heavy. Betty added, 'I have permission to tell you what the last test today is as you will not have to be monitored as such. You will be fitted with boots your size and will then be taken to a ladder that is fixed to one wall. This is a metal ladder and does not lean but goes straight up. It has 25 rungs. At the top you will have to climb inside a pod. You will have a safety line attached in case you have an accident, but I am sure you will have no trouble.' Her advice was to not look down.

She was not wrong about the weight of the boots. I was given a pair of fleecy socks and then sat down to put them on, followed by the boots. The boots clicked together and after Betty checked all was good, I clonked over to the ladder. This was a sight to behold, and both Betty and I were screaming with laughter by the time I reached the ladder. Especially when I found I could lean forward, and the boots stayed flat on the floor. (*Michael Jackson, eat your heart out.*) Once bent forward, I was unable to get back up. Betty rushed forward to help me, but as we were both giggling, she failed the first time. The second time, she pushed me too hard, and I swung upright, but then over backwards.

Johnny joined us, lifted me up and fitted a harness on me which attached to a rope over a pulley in the ceiling and called to one of his men to take the slack. I was facing the ladder and Johnny told me to start as soon as I felt ready. Taking a deep breath and holding onto the ladder, I lifted my left foot and placed it on the first rung.

Pushing with my right foot and pulling up with my arms, first rung was achieved. Then the second and then the third. I began to get rather cocky, thinking it was a piece of cake so to speak. Foolish, foolish woman. By the time I reached rung 15, my legs were shaking with the effort, and it felt like my arms were being pulled out of their sockets. 'Rest a while,' Johnny called, 'it's not a race.'

And a rest I took. I was breathing heavily and waited until it was nearly back to normal. Then off I set again. Left foot up, place, push with right, pull with arms. I made another eight rungs, only two left to go. I rested again, remembering I also had to climb into the pod.

'Final assault!' Johnny called. Right foot up, push with left, pull with arms. Left foot up, push with right, pull with arms. In front of me was an opening with grab rails each side of the opening. Leaning against the ladder, I reached for the rails, lifted my right foot, stepped onto the edge pushed with my left, and fell into the opening.

I lay on the floor of the pod breathing rather heavily. I heard Betty asking if I was ok, so I crawled to the opening and gave her the thumbs up. 'All you've got to do is get back down now, but you can take off the boots and climb down in your socks. Did I move, or did I move, I moved. Boots were unclicked and left in the pod and, as nimble as a gazelle I headed back down. Unfortunately, halfway my foot slipped and I began to fall. Luckily the man in charge of the harness was on the ball, and wrapped the rope around his body and arrested my fall. 'Phew!' I thought, that was close. The man continued to slowly lower me to the floor. Betty and Johnny were laughing, 'Well, that's one way to finish a test!' Johnny said.

Betty came to congratulate me, but I asked her to hang on for a minute and went across to thank the man on the harness. Betty introduced him as Airman Ben Dover. I thanked him for saving me, shook his hand, and Betty and Johnny told me I had ten minutes to get myself together and we would all be heading back to Base.

We returned to the main building in the black car that was once again surrounded by outriders. When we reached the main compound Betty told me to return to my room for about an hour she would call by and we could go to the Naafi together. Johnny headed off to the offices, I assumed to report the test results.

Chapter 10

I unlocked the door to my room and decided to have a quick freshen up. This didn't take long so, catching sight of the diary, I picked it up and sitting down in the armchair, started to read.

To my surprise, the name inside was not the one I expected. The first page read as follows: -

This diary belongs to

Esmerelda Verie Wanton

January 1835

'Goodness', I thought 'this is going to be fascinating. Wonder why this diary was among the things left by my parents. Settling myself comfortably in my chair I started to read.

1st day of January 1835

I just saw Harry Hardup at the New Year's Ball in Castle Cookenhousen, Count Spatula's country residence. There were over 200 guests, many of whom were staying at the castle. As we lived nearby at our country home, Hupdown House, we were able to travel to Castle Cooenkhousen easily. We arrived quite early. I was very excited as this was the first time we had been invited. My parents, Lord and Lady Muckenspreader had heard that Harry Hardup would be attending and told me I must not dance with him and not leave the ballroom with him. Mother added that he was looking for a rich wife as he had gambled his money away and other things not for my ears. I was an only child and had a very good dowry and it was inevitable that I would need to beware of fortune hunters. However, once I caught sight of Harry Hardup I fell instantly in love.

2nd day of January 1835

I danced with several men, a Baron or two and an aged Duke, but not Harry. He was busy flirting with the older spinsters who were known as being on the shelf. I felt pity for those women, but was annoyed Harry Hardup was wasting his time with them. After all, they were known as the Desperados for a reason. I spent the rest of the evening trying to think of a way to attract his attention, all to no avail.

3rd day of January 1835

I woke up this morning with a headache and a fever. My chest is hurting. The Doctor was called and I must stay I bed.

There was nothing further in the diary until ……

8th day of January 1835

I have been allowed downstairs today and spent the morning resting on the chaise longue supposedly reading a book but daydreaming about my dear Harry.

Mama told me the weather was about to change and snow was expected.

9th day of January 1835

Mama was right, we had a foot of snow overnight and it was still snowing.

10th day of January 1835

Snow now 2 feet deep

11th day of January 1835

I was by now fully recovered and Papa said that if it stopped snowing, in the morning he would arrange for me to be taken for a short ride in the sleigh.

12th day of January 1835

When I awoke, I rushed to the window to see whether it has stopped snowing. To my delight it had. I rang the bell for my maid, Mary.

'Quick,' I cried, 'help me get washed and dressed in warm clothes as I am going to be allowed out for a sleigh ride today.

I rushed down for breakfast and luckily Papa was still there. Sitting down at the table, I checked I was still allowed in the sleigh today. Papa told me he had ordered for it to be brought to the door at half past ten, so you have time to eat a good breakfast. At 10.25 of the clock I rushed upstairs to grab my warm cloak and muff. Lifting the hood of cloak over my hair I ran back downstairs just as the sleigh arrived. Our Butler, Heaves, opened the door for me and wished me a happy ride.

We had been out for about 15 minutes, when we met up with several people from Castle Cookenhauson. The women were also in a sleigh and the men were riding beside it. Harry was amongst them. The men dismounted and bowed towards me. 'Well met,' Harry said, 'we were just on our way to invite you to my engagement party. Marianna Croesus has done the honour of agreeing to become my bride. I couldn't believe this, Marianna was one of the spinsters, who was at least 22 years of age. She didn't laugh, she tittered in the most annoying way. She sat in the sleigh smirking at me, and I had to fight back my tears. Thinking quickly, I congratulated them both but told them my Mama had contracted a fever and was laid up in bed. Therefore, we would be unable to attend the party. Harry came over to my sleigh and bowed once again. As he did so, he put his hand into his pocket to get his glove and his handkerchief fell from the same pocket straight into my sleigh. I didn't say anything about it but asked my driver to take me home. When we were out of the sight of the others I bent down and picked up his handkerchief and saw it had HH embroidered in the corner.

13th Day of January 1835

My heart is broken, I will never marry.

Those were the last words written in the diary. Perhaps I will search the internet to see if I can find out more about Esmerelda Verie Wanton.

Chapter 11

I was busy reading when Betty arrived. 'Ready?' she asked when I went to answer it. 'I surely am.' I replied and grabbing my bag and door key I joined her for the short walk to the Naafi. I started to tell her about the diary and told her she was welcome to read it. 'Yes please,' she replied, 'I could turn it into one of my books, I will send you a copy. We were both laughing at the thought when we entered the Naafi. We went straight to the dining room and chose a table a little apart from other diners. Sitting down, I wondered which waiter would be coming to take our orders. We picked up a menu to decide what we would choose. We didn't have either the lisper or the stutterer. We had a waitress. Her identity pass showed her name to be Goldie Gobbogobber and boy, did she live up to her name.

'Wotcha want?' she demanded, 'Specials tunite are mine strone soup, Usses n fries and Choclat fudge cake wiv cussard. To cut a long discussion short I asked for all three specials. With a quick glance at me, Betty said she would have the same.

'Rightho, that's two mine strone, two Uss n fries and two choclat fudge cakes wiv custard.

'Wot ya want ta drink?' I asked for tea and Betty a white wine. One tea and white wine was added.

Off she stomped and we heard her shout when she went through the door into the kitchen area, two mine strones, two usses n fries and two choc fudges.

We both burst out laughing. 'Well,' Betty said, 'makes a change from lisping or stuttering. I can't wait for her to bring our mine strone, and I wonder whether we will also get a roll and butter, or should that be bu—er?' We didn't have to wait long to find out. Goldie was heading towards us carrying a tray with our mine strone n rolls n bu—er. Off she sashayed towards the bar where she flirted with the barman for several minutes before getting my tea and requesting a glass of wine. Betty leaned towards me and told me the barman is Chris Cross III and is the son of Air Chief Marshal Chris Cross II. He is working at the bar as a punishment after he got very drunk with friends one night and stole the keys to his father's private helicopter. They all climbed inside the helicopter and Chris flew it up straight into some power lines. Luckily it was not that high so although it crashed nobody was seriously hurt, However, it did cause a blackout across the Air force base and several villages and towns nearby. He was arrested for flying under the influence of alcohol, has his licence taken away for 2 years. He was fined £5,000 and must carry out 200 hours of community service. Working at the bar is a further punishment imposed on him by his father.

What community work has he done so far?' I asked. 'Well, so far, he has had to go along the grass verges with several other guys doing community service. They must wear fluorescent orange jackets with Community Payback on the back for everyone to see. They have litter picker uppers and sacks to put the litter in. He has also had to clean graffiti off walls and weed and tidy the gardens in the park. His friend also got 100 hours community work each, but they are not allowed to work together. 'No wonder he is miserable.' I thought.

By now we had finished our mine strones and awaited Goldie's return. She was busy gathering bowls and plates from other tables, so I took the opportunity to ask Betty what would be happening next. She told me tomorrow would be a day off for me, but the next day I would be taken back to the examination area where I would be told what the experience is. I could either agree to it or decline. If I decided against it, I would be given a cheque for £1,000.

At that moment, Goldie arrived at our table and removed the soup dishes and plates, informing us she would be right back with our Usses. Of course, she detoured past the bar to flirt with Chris Cross, who decided at that point to disappear down the steps to the cellar. Goldie was now very miffed, which didn't bode well for her attitude therefrom.

Betty and I watched this with not a little smile as Goldie entered the kitchen. Not two minutes later she returned with our mains. 'Two Usses n fries,' she said slapping them down on the table before us. 'Anyfing else ya want?' she asked. I got quite daring and asked for mayo and tartare sauce. *(If looks could kill, I would have been struck dead where I sat.)* Without another word she stomped over to the service table, grabbed the mayo and sauce, and returned to our table and chucked down the sachets. Betty and I concentrated on our Usses for a while, not looking at each other in case we started to laugh at Goldie's temper tantrum. The fries were amazingly tasty and the batter on the Usses was the best I have ever had.

Now feeling fat and full, we sat back again awaiting the arrival of Goldie to collect our plates. Unexpectedly she was smiling. 'Did yer enjoy em?' she asked. I'll go and get yer fudges.' 'Well,' I said to Betty, 'Do you think she has scored with Chris Cross II?' 'No,' she replied, 'look over by the serving table.' And there was Goldie chatting away to my saviour, Ben Down. He really was so handsome, piercing blue eyes and black curly hair that fell over his forehead making one's fingers itch to run your fingers through it. As for his smile, even my heart skipped a beat. 'Guess we will be waiting a while for our fudges.' I thought. But no, Goldie suddenly left for the kitchen. Ben poured himself a coffee and strolled over to a cosy area that had a television and several armchairs with small tables beside them. He chose one where he could see what was going on in the dining room.

Not long after Goldie was heading towards our table with a tray and our fudges. 'Ere's yer fudges,' she said, putting them down in front of us, 'I've gotten a date this evenin' wiv a very dreamy fella!' We both smiled and wished her well. She waved at Ben before going to another table to clear away. 'We'd better eat our fudges as quickly as we can, so we don't stand in the way of the new romance.' Said Betty grinning. I suggested she should take notes for her next book. She could call it 'Love Reaches Boiling Point Over Usses n Fries.' Or 'It was all down to the Mine Strone.'

After our meal we decided to go for a stroll to stretch our legs before bedtime. There was a park attached to the Base that was lit by old fashioned lamp posts. I noticed several benches strategically placed around a small lake. Turning a corner, we caught sight of Ben and Gloria huddled together on one of the benches. Was young love blossoming?

We left the park and walked back to the living area where my room was situated. 'Have you thought what you will do tomorrow?' asked Betty. There are horse riding stables just down the road where you could book a ride, or you could go into town and mosey around the shops, or both if you feel like it. You can catch a bus just outside the Base that passes the stables and goes into Oldnewtown town centre. If you ask the bus driver, he will happily stop at the stables to let you out. The buses run every half an hour, so you aren't tied to a particular time to go.' I decided to wait until the morning and see how I felt. After wishing Betty a good night, I unlocked the door to my room and decided to go straight to bed.

Chapter 12

I had a bit of a lay in in the morning. Eventually I got up and rang for a pot of tea and scrambled eggs on toast. I put on my dressing gown, and it wasn't too long before there was a knock on my door. Paul Patterthon, his name tag showed, greeted me with, 'Good morning, here ith your tea and thcramblede eggth on toatht. Enjoy - I will collect the tray later, jutht leave it outthide your door.' I thanked him smiling to myself.

After breakfast I had a shower and dressed in jeans and a jumper. It was sunny, but there was a cold breeze. I decided I would go horse riding and take it from there. As I had no idea what the bus times were, I strolled out of the base and saw several people waiting by the bus stop. As I joined them, we greeted each other with 'Good Mornings' and I asked about how long the bus would be. One bright spark told me it would be about 50 feet. That broke the ice, and everyone began chatting and I was told it would be along any minute now. When I said where I was hoping to go, I was told to let the driver know I wanted to be put down outside of Plodders Farm Equestrian Centre.

The bus duly arrived – it had 20 seats, 7 of which were already taken. I got on last and asked the driver to please stop at Plodders Farm. He nodded and asked or £1 for my fare. I found a seat next to a window and settled down to enjoy the journey. The chatter went on around me, but I was content just to listen. We drove through a small hamlet named Little Booby, which made me smile. Next was a dairy farm I think, as there were cows in several fields. I couldn't quite see the full name, but it ended 'cowsanbulls.' I made to note to look again on my return journey.

'Coming up to Plodders Farm.' the driver called, slowing the bus down. I quickly rose and went to the door, which was now open. Thanking the driver, I got off the bus and waited until it drove away. I had to cross the road to go into Plodders Farm Equestrian Centre. I walked up the drive and saw a sign for the stables. 'Here goes,' I thought and walked toward what looked like an office. I knocked on the door and was asked to enter. A woman sat behind a desk (well I think it was a desk, I couldn't see it for the books, papers, half eaten sandwiches, a bridle with a leading rope, etc) and looking up asked how she could help. I replied that I was staying at the Airforce Base and heard you give riding lessons and as it was something I had always wanted to do, but never got round to, I thought now would be a good time to try. Rising to her feet, she held out her hand, which I took and shook. 'I'm Agatha Twisty, but I'm known as Saggy Aggy, Saggy for short. (I wondered how she could be so casual about her nickname, which I felt was rather unkind.) She must have read my mind, because she said, 'It's left over from my childhood when I had to wear clothes that were too big for me and always sagged down past my knees.' 'Oh,' I replied, 'that's a relief.' She explained it would cost £10 an hour as I wouldn't be galloping, probably not even cantering. I felt that was very reasonable and took the money out of my purse to give to her. I asked if I could leave my coat and handbag here and she put my bag into a small safe and locked the door. She then asked me to follow her to the stables, so we could look over the horses to see which one would be suitable for a learner.

I was very impressed with the stables; the horses were obviously very well loved. When they heard us coming, they popped their heads over the stable half doors, whinnying. She first went into a spare stable and grabbed a couple of riding hats, one of which she plumped on my head. It was a little on the large side, and when I turned my head, the hat stayed still. 'Hey ho.' I thought to myself, tightening up the strap and hoping for the best. Saggy moved along fussing each horse as she passed. She stopped in front of a bay horse whose name was painted above the door – Petal - and stroked her nose (Petal's not her own.) 'This lovely lady will give you a nice ride.' she said. (I was unsure whether she was referring to me or the horse.) So saying, she led Petal out of her stall and put on her saddle and bridle, etc. She then went to another stall, stroked the nose of another horse, Hercules, and tacked that horse up too. She led my horse to a mounting block and explained how to get aboard. She shortened the stirrups, showed me how to hold the reins, then mounted Hercules and instructed me to follow her. Luckily Petal knew what to do and placidly followed in Hercules path. Soon we came to a twitten which led up to a hill and Petal decided to test my mettle! First, she rubbed along a hedge of Hawthorn bushes and brambles, which was a little on the prickly side, and when, on instruction from Saggy, I pulled the right-hand rein to get her away from the hedge, she decided to walk along the edge of the path, which had a nasty drop down to the ground below. Thankfully we soon got to the hills and Saggy suggested we tried trotting. (If you don't know what trotting entails, it takes a lot of upping and downing in tune with the horse.) Before us there was a path that led up a large mound, and another that led around it. Saggy started her horse trotting and Petal followed suit. She then started to call, up/down, up/down, up/down.

Don't worry she called Petal will follow me. (*I think you know what is coming next.*) Yes, she and Hercules followed the lower path and Petal, and I went up the large mound. I upped and downed as best I could as her voice got further and further away.

As luck would have it the lower path joined up with the upper path and we came together once more. We continued to up and down for a while until we came to a gate. Saggy opened the gate which revealed a stony path leading downwards. I was told to close the gate behind me and follow her down. The stones were loose and moved about and Petal and I sort of slid downwards. I was now riding cowboy style, stirrups out in front while I leaned back. My hat decided to fall backwards on my head, causing me to choke. I reached up and pulled it back on properly. At last, we reached our starting point, but unfortunately the horses knew they were close to their stables and sped up to what I guess was canter speed. I had to duck under tree branches to avoid being left hanging from them by my neck.

To say I was relieved to get off that horse is an understatement. (I didn't get off, I fell.) Saggy smiled at me, saying I had done very well and recommended I continued learning to ride. 'Oh, I will' I said, wobbling back towards the office. My bag was returned to me, and I quickly hightailed it back up the drive to the road. Luckily there was a bench on the other side of the road opposite the farm and I gratefully sank down on it.

Chapter 13

I checked the time on my watch. Unbelievably it was only 12.30pm. I got up and walked about a bit and found only my posterior was hurting. That being the case I decided I would go into Oldnewtown and find somewhere to have lunch. After a few minutes I could see the bus coming down the road and I stood at the kerb and put my hand out as I was unsure whether the driver would stop otherwise. The bus slowed down and stopped, and the driver opened the door. 'Good afternoon,' I said, I would like to go to Oldnewtown centre please.' 'That'll be £1.50 madam' he answered and went on to say, 'The bus goes straight to the terminal in the town centre, so stay on the bus until then.' Thanking him I paid my £1.50 and walked to the back of the bus in search of a window seat, as the bus was almost full. I signed with relief as I found one and sat down. Off we trundled, the chattering started up, something I was not used to where I come from. They really were a friendly lot down here. I learned a woman had had washing stolen of her line, little Jimmy Piddleton had broken his leg after falling out of a tree while scrumping, and Mrs Looselegs had given birth to her ninth child. 'Goodness,' I thought, 'I could write a book about what I have heard over the last few days!'

After a few minutes I tuned out of the conversations and gazed out at the passing scenery. Small clusters of houses dotted the route. Some had thatched roofs while others were just tiled. We passed a Cottage that was all on its own and which was full of colour in the garden from the profusion of flowers growing. The bus slowed to a stop just past the cottage and one of the women got out. She was carrying a large flat wicker basket. Then I saw there was a car park by the cottage, which was called 'Heavenly Flowers.' There was also an entrance through a large gateway and above it was a sign stating P Y O heavenly blooms. Prices vary, ask Dolly Daydream, who will be happy to escort you around. What a lovely place I thought, I would love to just walk around all those beautiful flowers.

As we drove away one of the other passengers remarked that Mrs Bloomsbury must be running out of potpourri if she's gone into Heavenly Blooms. She continued, 'My sister-in-law bought some from her at the Market and she told me it is really good.'

Another passenger asked what market she was at. 'The one in Port Tidal, it's there every Thursday morning. I'm going next week if you would like to come with me. I usually catch the eight am bus, which will get us there by nine, that way we will beat the crowds and can be on our way home by eleven. I also go to the Bert's Fresh Meat van to buy my meat for the week. I highly recommend Bert's Bangers and Beefburgers. Last week I bought a nice piece of lamb for our Sunday lunch. It just fell apart when cooked. A couple of the other passengers also wanted to go, and one suggested making a day of it, they could have lunch out and go for a stroll along the seafront before returning home. (Oh, how I wished I could join them – this place was casting a spell over me.)

By now we were entering a more built-up area, and I noticed everyone was gathering themselves together. Before long we entered the bus depot and the others alighted. I asked the driver what times the buses were back to the Base, and he gave me a timetable, which showed the buses depart every half hour. Getting off the bus I made my way to the main street of Oldnewtown. It was rather busy, but not uncomfortably so. Turning left I strolled along admiring the shops and doing a bit of window shopping. While peering through another shop window I could see tables and chairs. The tables were covered with crisp white cloths. I stepped back and looked up and saw the place was called Forgetmenot Tea Shoppe. That sounded so pretty I decided I would go in and perhaps get something for my lunch. A smiling woman was standing behind the counter and she invited me to choose a table and she would give me time to read the menu and would then come and take my order. I sat down at a table or two and looked at the menu. Straight away I saw it was going to be hard to choose.

Menu

Welsh Rarebit with crisps - £2.50

Beans on Toast - £2.50

Baked Potato with Coleslaw - £2.50

Baked potato with Grated Cheese - £2.50

Baked potato with Tuna and sweetcorn - £2.50

Toasted Teacake with butter - £2.50

Homemade Scone with butter, jam, and clotted cream - £2.50

Slice of Lemon Drizzle Cake - £2.50

Slice of Chocolate Cake - £2.50

Slice of Victoria Sponge - £2.50

Slice of date and walnut cake - £2.50

Pot of tea for one - £2.50

Pot of Coffee for one - £2.50

I finally selected what I would like and waved at the owner, who introduced herself as Aunty Aspicety. She was wearing a white frilly apron over a pretty summer dress. I ordered a Welsh Rarebit, a piece of date cake and a pot of tea. I hadn't realised how hungry I was because it didn't take long to eat my Welsh Rarebit and move on to my cake. I poured myself a cup of tea and noticed the teapot, cups, and saucers, even the sugar and milk jug all matched and were decorated with forget-me-nots. Gazing around the tearoom I noticed there were also mugs for sale with the same pattern, and, yes, they were also £2.50 each. I decided I would buy 2 mugs too - I could give one to Betty and keep one or myself. 'I must find something for Johnny.' I thought. Having finished my cake, I paid my bill which in total came to £12.50 and left a tip for Aunty Aspicety, and returned outside, in search of something suitable or Johnny. A few shops along I saw an old-fashioned sweet shop called Bountiful Bonbons. There were so many jars of sweets that brought back happy memories. Knowing I would be sure to find something in here for Johnny, I entered the shop and the first thing that caught my eye was a jar of Flying Saucers. 'Hmm,' I thought, 'a few of those would do.' But then I saw the Gobstoppers. 'Oh yes, must have one of those and a bag of Flying Saucers. I placed my order with the happy looking man behind the counter and left, feeling rather chuffed with my purchases.

Glancing at my watch, I realised it was time to get back to the Bus Depot and return to the Base in time to get ready for the evening meal. Not that I will be that hungry, but I would be able to give Betty and Johnny their presents.

Chapter 14

I walked quickly back to the Bus Depot and was pleased to see the bus I needed to get waiting there. It was the same driver who had brought me here, and he asked if I had enjoyed myself. Of course, I told him I had a wonderful time. I paid my fare and found a seat quite close to the front of the bus. I saw a couple of the women who had travelled on the same bus as me on the way to Oldnewhampton who were sitting together. Their bags were full and looked very heavy. I heard one of them say she had bought her Alf a bag of Jap Desserts and the kids Sherbert Fountains from Bountiful Bonbons. She had got herself some Winter Mixture, adding that she loved the ones with chewy centres.

Another three people got on the bus, one of whom was Ben Dover. As he went to pass by me, he realised who I was and asked if he could sit next to me. I replied that of course he could. It was rather nice to have someone to chat to. I asked him how his romance was going with Goldie (*I know it was a bit cheeky to ask this, but nothing ventured nothing gaine*d.) I was pleased to hear that they were going to the cinema at the weekend. Unfortunately, he had duties to perform, so apart from having a quick word with each other when they were both in the Naafi, they had to wait until then. He told me that Goldie may seem to be loud and pushy, but she is really a very sweet person. I find it difficult to talk to other people, especially women, so there are no embarrassing pauses while I try to think of something to say, Goldie fills in the silence no trouble at all. 'She is working tonight, and I have bought her a little gift, would you mind giving to her for me? I will be away for a couple of days, so cannot do it myself. I am heading out in an hour or so.' Of course, I was more than happy to do that for him, and he made me look at Goldie in an entirely different light. I told him I would be more than happy to do that for him.

We stopped talking for a while and spent time looking out the window. Meanwhile, the women were still gossiping. I whispered in Ben's ear, 'Listen to the ladies, you never know what you might hear.' I am so pleased we listened, cos one lady mentioned she found out her husband was having an affair with his secretary, so she cut all his clothes in half, put them in a suitcase and left them on the front lawn. She had the locks changed and got her two brothers to come and stay with her, one of whom was a retired boxer. (She had obviously been planning this for some time, as she had cleaned out their joint bank account and appointed a solicitor to work on her behalf.)

We stopped at the next bus stop, and the driver turned round and asked what happened when her husband returned home. By now, we were all nodding our heads and encouraging her to finish her story. All heads were turned in her direction, and realising this was her moment of glory, she added. 'Well, it was rather late when he got home, after a long meeting at work (she said sarcastically) so he didn't see the case but walked up to the door and put his key in the lock. (There was a group sound of indrawn breaths) …. the woman was obviously enjoying herself, as we all leaned further forward to hear the next part of the story. And we waited and waited a bit more. 'Jane! Tell us what happened next, or we might just have to smack you!' (That made me smile, as the woman who was going to smack her was half Jane's size. However, I digress.) 'So,' Jane went on to say, 'He was slightly worse for wear, and tried several times to turn the lock. My brothers and I were waiting on the inside by the front door, and when he started flapping the letterbox and shouting through it, my boxing brother slipped his hand through the letterbox and grabbed hold of the cheating brutes tie, pulling it back through the letterbox. Robert (her husband) started to make choking noises, and gasped 'What the hell is going on here? Let me in this instance.' My other brother opened the door, while my boxing brother still held tightly to his tie. By now half the neighbourhood were looking out their windows or even standing in their front gardens, shouting to each other, and cheering when they saw the door open and Robert having to move with it. Finally, my brother let go of his tie and Robert staggered back. 'What the hell is going on?' he shouted, 'have you lost your mind?' Knowing my brothers would keep him away from me, I told him I had known of his affair with his secretary for some time and I had taken steps to ensure I was not going to lose and allow the homewrecker to grab their joint money as well as him. Not that he was much of a bargain. She took great delight in informing him she had cleaned out their joint account, and as he had put the house in her, Jane's, name, he could go and get his suitcase and go move in with the homewrecker. She added she had also maxed out his credit card. He started to beg her to forgive him, saying it was all a dreadful mistake, but she told her brothers to escort him off the premises. He is going to try to fight it in court, but he doesn't stand much chance.

By now we were all cheering and congratulating her, and the bus driver suddenly realised we were running behind time. 'Hold on to your hats!' he shouted, 'we are going to speed up a little to make up some time.' Speed up a little! Without a word of a lie, we must have hit seventy m.p.h. at least. We were all laughing and cheering the driver on. As I have said before, I was beginning to wish I lived here among these wonderful people.

Chapter 15

It wasn't long before we passed Plodders Farm. 'That's a place I won't miss.' I thought. Further on there was a signpost saying Little Booby and I remembered I wanted to see what the full name of the farm was. The bus slowed and came to a stop and the farm came into view. I saw it was called Great Cowsanbulls. The lady who had purchased sweets from Bountiful Bonbons got off the bus and after waving goodbye to her friends, walked towards the lane leading to the farm. A young boy came running towards her, gesturing towards her bag. She stopped and took out the bag of sweets and removed a Sherbert Fountain and gave it to him. Putting her arm around his shoulder she hugged him to her and then together they continued walking along the lane to the farm. For some reason that brought tears to my eyes, and I quickly wiped them away, telling myself I was just tired.

'Airforce Base' the driver called, and Ben and I rose to our feet. Ben offered me a hand down off the bus. We walked up to the buildings together and, at a fork in the road, Ben turned and thanked me again for giving the present to Goldie, adding that he had to go the other way to me. Checking I had Goldie's gift, I continued up the road to the building housing my room. Reaching in my bag for the key, I quickly unlocked my door, slipping my shoes off and putting my bag of the bed. I decided to take a quick shower and put on a dress for a change. I hadn't long been ready before there was a familiar knocking on my door. I unlocked the opened the door welcomed Betty inside.

'How did your day go?' she asked. 'Brilliantly,' I replied, 'I have so much to tell you. 'Do you know who is taking dinner orders tonight', I asked. Betty said she thought it was Goldie as she passed her on the way to see me, and she was wearing her waitress outfit. Clapping my hands together I asked whether it would be ok for us to order something to be delivered here, we could sit at the table outside and enjoy the evening sunshine. Like I said, I have so much to tell you and, Ben Down, who is on his way somewhere under orders, caught the same bus home as me and asked if I would give Goldie a gift from him with his love. They have another date at the weekend, but he wanted her to know he would be thinking of her.'

I also asked if Johnny was around this evening. Betty offered to give him a ring to find out. He was, so I asked her to invite him to share a meal with us here. Johnny said he was at a loose end and would be happy to join us.

Betty and I took turns looking through the menu while we waited for Johnny. We both found it difficult to choose, we didn't want a huge meal, but not a small one either. There was another knock at the door. 'That must be Johnny.' Betty said, getting up to let him in. 'Good evening, ladies.' he said, to what do I owe the pleasure of your invitation?' Smiling at him, I replied, 'I thought it would be nice to have a meal together, as I feel we have become friends. I know I have a decision to make tomorrow but that is tomorrow. We have been trying to decide what to order from the menu and neither of us can decide. We are eating it here because I have a special duty to perform for Ben Dover.' I went on to explain about the budding romance between Ben and Goldie.

'Why don't we order a Chinese takeaway?' suggested Johnny, 'We can get our drinks from the bar in the dining room and ask that Goldie bring them over.' 'Now, what a good idea,' said Betty, there is a Chinese Takeaway in Port Tidal. I can get the menu on my phone. Shall we order a mixture of dishes, and we can then help ourselves to what we like. We can share the cost three ways. 'I readily agreed to this and reminded them we would need plates and cutlery. 'No worries, I will ask for them at the same time as ordering our drinks.'

I left it to the two of them to decide what to order, hoping Johnny had a big appetite, as they ordered several different dishes. Johnny paid for the food using his bank card and then asked what drinks we would like. Betty suggested we order a bottle of white wine to be shared between us. Johnny phoned through to the bar in the dining room, asked for a bottle of white wine, a couple of beers for himself and requested plates a cutlery to be sent over. He stressed he wanted Goldie to bring them to my room, but she was not to be given it all on one tray. The drinks first and then the rest on another tray. We asked for the drinks to be put down to visitor entertainment. He looked at us and grinned, 'Got to have some perks.'

Betty went outside to make sure the table and chairs were clean enough to use. Johnny joined her and sat I the first chair she had cleaned. As we had about half an hour until the food arrived, I quickly grabbed my bag and took out the mug and the sweets. I hadn't thought about wrapping them up, so I wrapped them in a paper tissue. It was rather obvious what Betty's gift was, but Johnny's looked quite intriguing. Then I grabbed the glass tumbler from the bathroom, half filled it with water and then went outside to pick some wildflowers, arranged them in the tumbler and placed them in the centre of the table. 'Very nice touch.' Complimented Johnny, who was happily smoking a pipe, looking at peace with the world.

Betty had disappeared, but she returned shortly carrying a Citronella candle which she asked Johnny to light and then also placed it on the table. I opened the door to my room so Goldie could come straight in with our drinks. It wasn't long before she arrived. I took the tray from her which I noted had the glasses and she turned to get our plates and cutlery. I placed the wine bottle and beer cans on the table and left Johnny to do the honours.

I went back inside and grabbed the gift for Goldie from Ben and the ones I had bought for them. I placed theirs in front of them and put Goldie's next to the spare chair. I sat down and requested them to open their presents. 'Oh,' exclaimed Betty, tongue in cheek, 'I wonder what mine is!' We all laughed as she unwrapped it, and I produced mine to show we both had the same one. I just fell in love with them I told her. Betty got up and gave me a big hug. 'I love it too,' she said, 'I will think of you every time I use it. Turning to Johnny, I told him that as I didn't think he would want a mug with Forgetmenots on it, I got him something he could enjoy now. He had been poking at it trying to work out what it was. I laughingly told him to stop poking and unwrap it. When he saw what he had, he burst out laughing, saying he loved flying saucers and had no idea the round thing was a gobstopper. Betty informed him that if he got too out of hand this evening, he would have it shoved into his mouth to stop him. We were still laughing when Goldie returned. She came outside to the table and started to place our plates and cutlery on the table. I asked her to sit down for a moment and handed her the gift from Ben. I explained that he had caught the same bus home from

Newoldtown as me and had asked me to give it to her as he would be away from the Base for a couple of days and hadn't had time to see her. He wanted her to know he was thinking of her.

Goldie unwrapped the gift and clasped the box inside to her heart. 'Open it, we can't wait to see what's inside.' Betty said. Goldie took the lid off the box revealing a beautiful silver chain bracelet with a heart in the middle. Goldie took it out of the box and asked Betty to help her put it on. It was so delicate and fit her so well. By now we were all wiping tears from our eyes, even Johnny, who said he had smoke in his eyes from his pipe. Goldie sat there looking at the bracelet on her wrist and said she had never met a man who was as kind and caring as Ben. He was like a dream come true. Then she jumped to her feet and said she must get back to the dining room, thanked us all, and with a final sniff hurried off. 'Bless her.' I said, 'I don't think anyone has ever given her a present before.

Johnny had already started to eat his flying saucers; he was obviously very hungry. While we were waiting for our Chinese to arrive, I told them all about my day. Both Betty and Johnny really laughed at my description of Saggy Aggy and my subsequent ride. 'I never want to hear up down up down ever again,' I said, 'I think the large hat would even have been too big for you Johnny. They were even more interested in the woman who caught her husband cheating. I had just reached the part where the bus driver started speeding when our Chinese arrived. I couldn't believe how much Johnny had ordered. I had balanced the plates on the radiator to warm them up and put them onto the table using the hand towel from the bathroom. We used our dessert spoons to dish up our choices. Johnny had poured us another glass of wine and himself a beer, and we raised our glasses 'to friendship and tomorrow.'

What a lovely evening we had, I ate more than I thought possible, but it was all so delicious. Johnny ordered us another bottle of wine and a brandy for himself. We had laughed so much my cheeks ached. Luckily, there was nobody else staying in the complex where my room was because we got louder and louder. I had found some disco music on my mobile and we danced around like teenagers. It was about 10pm when we noticed we had attracted an audience. Goldie, Tim, Paul and even Chris III came. 'Come in' called Johnny, 'help yourself to some left over Chinese. (As you probably know, nobody turns down Chinese food, even if it is cold.)

Of course, the youngsters showed us their dances and at one point I found myself doing Northern Soul to some Jazz Funk group. On realising it was now well past midnight, we called a halt to the festivities. It took us half an hour to clear up, and Chris III offered to return the plates, cutlery, and glasses to the kitchen for us on his way home. There were hugs all round and Johnny said we would have our Meeting at 11.am in the morning to allow us to clear our heads first. I waved everyone off, drank a glass of water, quickly got undressed and fell into bed.

Chapter 16

Tomorrow has come!

I awoke at 9.30am. Luckily, I didn't have a bad headache, just a niggle. Carefully rising from the bed, I went into the bathroom for a shower. Today I am back to jeans and a jumper. For some reason I was feeling apprehensive. Before going across to the dining room for breakfast I made myself a cup of tea and went to sit at the table outside and slowly sipped it, breathing in the fresh air. I went back inside and took a couple of headache pills.

'OK,' I said to myself, time to head over for breakfast. I didn't want to be late for the meeting. As I didn't want a large breakfast, I went to the self-service area and got a cup of tea and a piece of toast. I sat down at a nearby table and was just spreading butter on my toast when I heard 'It's much, much, much too early!' Looking up I smiled at Betty, who was dressed in full uniform and looking rather green about the gills. 'Oh dear, that bad, is it?' I asked, 'here, take a couple of these.' She sat down and I handed her the headache pills and got up to get her a glass of water. I made her a slice of toast, which I handed to her suggesting she eat it without butter. I asked if we were back to formality today and she nodded her head. We sat quietly for a while and all that could be heard was the crunching of toast. I glanced at my watch and noticed it was now 10.50am and asked what happens next. We were to meet Johnny outside at 11.00am and we would once again take a car with an escort to the same building where I took my tests, but in a different area.

Promptly at 11.00 we stood outside waiting for Johnny and the car. It soon arrived and the back door was opened by a man in uniform. As I climbed in, I saw Johnny sitting on the seat with his back to the driver. Betty and I sat facing the front. 'Good morning, Sir.' I said. He smiled at me and asked if I was ready for today. I told him I couldn't answer that until I knew what my choices would be, making him laugh.

This time we were taken to a different door. As we exited the car, I saw the words 'Top Secret' written on the folder Johnny had under his arm. Another officer approached carrying an Attaché case with a lock on it and he led us into the building. We approached a screening area and I had to stop to have photographs taken, full and side faced. We had to wait a few minutes until a pass was handed to me. It had a lanyard attached and I was told to wear it around my neck the whole time I was in the building.

We were then taken to a meeting room. There were screens around the room, two of which had security cameras outside the building attached. These were being monitored by two men wearing headphones. They had a type of joystick which enabled them to turn the cameras in a search mode. Johnny bent down and quietly informed me they were known as Tweedlesee and Tweedlesaw. When I asked which was which, he replied he was not sure as they were identical twins, which made me giggle.

We walked to a table that was on the other side of the room. Johnny pulled out a chair for me and he then sat down at the head of the table. There was a flask of water and glasses on the table. Betty poured us all a drink from the flask and sat down opposite me. The Officer with the Attaché case came into the room and placed it on the table in front of Johnny. He then left. Johnny entered a code on the Attaché case and opened it. He took out several papers and some photographs and placed them on the table, putting the case down on the floor.

I will be explaining what this is all about, but firstly I need you to sign the Official Secrets Act. He passed the paper to me and asked me to read it through thoroughly and then sign it. While I was reading Betty went to a table with cups, a jug of milk and a large flask full of hot water. She made me a cup of tea and coffee for herself and Johnny. She placed our drinks in front of us and sat back down.

Having read the Official Secrets Act through, I signed as requested. I handed it back to Johnny and he asked whether I had decided to take the money, or whether I had decided to go ahead with the, yet unknown experience. I was about to speak when Johnny held up his hand. He said he thought it only fair that I know what that would be.

He then showed me photographs of a large drone, which could reach top speeds of 200 mph. He pointed out the cabin underneath the drone. This cabin can hold three people. One person to take control of the drone, one person to take photographs of the land we are covering when the drone is put into hovering mode. The third person would usually be from the military who is carrying out special orders.

Although we have tested the drone, we need further tests to be carried out. Presently we do not want knowledge of this project to be leaked to the outside world. We have great plans for this drone. It could be used by all the arms of our forces. The army could use it for the rescue of men caught behind enemy lines for example, the navy could use it in place of helicopters when speed was of the essence, keeping track of enemy shipping above or below the water. And we will be using it for many things. Instead of sending, say Ben Dover, to collect papers, orders, etc, which can sometimes take days, we can send him by Drone and he could be there and back the same day or couple of hours, depending on the distance.

The trial we will be undertaking, and which involves you, is a test run. We will not be taking this drone up today. However, you will be given training on rappelling down a rope, then putting on a harness at speed and climbing a kinetic ladder back into the drone. The harness is a form of safety net, should you somehow slip off the ladder. If this happens, you will be wound up electronically. This harness can also be used with a cage attachment so if we were picking up a handler and his dog that had been sent in to track a criminal, both the man and the dog would be safe. It can also be loaded with anything that would fit.

So, you will be practising this afternoon in the special facility inside the compound. The reason for this is the secrecy aspect. Tomorrow we will be driven to Salisbury Plains where the drone is in storage and guarded day and night. I will be the pilot and Betty will be taking the photographs and lowering the ladder and harness. What we need you to remember, if you agree to take part in this trial, is that you must allow the rope ladder to be grounded before you climb it or you will get an electric shock. We will need you to climb the ladder as quickly as you can.

If you get on well tomorrow, there will be another trial to take part in. I will tell you about this after tomorrow's trial.

'What I need to add,' he said, is that we won't always be taking military people and this is why we needed to search for a healthy person to undertake the tests you passed, so we can gain the knowledge we need for the future. As this drone can reach very high speeds, we need to know how a fit person would react under these, particularly if you are sent straight down to the ground. Particularly a woman.'

He fell silent, giving me time to think. And think I did. I felt rather excited, but also a little fearful at the same time. I looked at Betty, then at Johnny, who were looking back at me, and made a decision. I told them I would like to go ahead, providing I managed to conquer rappelling, donning a harness, and climbing a ladder. Johnny stood and offered his hand for a handshake. Betty ran round the table and gave me a big hug. Johnny then took a bottle of champagne from a fridge by the service table and. Betty produced three glasses and we raised our glasses to each other.

As it was now lunch time, we left the room and were taken to the dining room inside the building. This was self service and we queued up with the others and helped ourselves to what we wanted. Johnny piled his plate up high with meat pie and vegetables. Betty had quiche and salad and a baked potato. I chose crispy chicken in lemon sauce and rice. As we headed towards a table, Johnny and Betty received many hi's and hello's which they happily returned. When we had eaten our main, we again returned to the self-service for a sweet course. We all chose lemon meringue pie and cream. As we passed the drinks station, we collected a drink at the same time. I chose water, Betty had coffee and Johnny went for a glass of orange juice.

Chapter 17

When we had finished eating, Johnny suggested we take a stroll around the airfield attached to the building to help our food go down.

After fifteen minutes he led us towards a large hanger near the main building and Johnny took us to the small door, which was in a huge door. He explained the large door slides open to allow the helicopter to fly out. The building was very tall, and I noticed high platforms with ladders leading up to them. There were also ropes hanging down to the floor. Further round there were kinetic ladders, and, of course, harnesses. An instructor came walking towards us. Johnny introduced him to me. 'This is Flying Officer Skipson Roper, Skip for short. We shook hands and so the training began.

Skip picked up a harness and instructed me to stand in it. He then attached other pieces of equipment to the harness and walked me to a rope that was fixed to the ceiling and the floor. (*I want you to imagine how stupid I looked, trying to walk in a harness with a piece of rope with attachments hanging between my legs.*) I heard Betty snigger. I shot her a dirty look, which only made her laugh more.) When I finally reached the rope, he showed me how to attach the rope thingy hanging between my legs to it. I nodded, trying to look intelligent, and he then put this ring thingy in my hand and explained I hold this in one hand, and guide myself down using the other when rappelling. He unhooked it from the rope and asked me to step out of the harness. He instructed me to watch him rappel. So, I did! He climbed up onto one of the high platforms, stepped into a harness, attached the other regalia, and stepped off the platform. He lowered himself slowly shouting out what he was doing as he descended. I can only say how brilliant he was at rappelling!

He then climbed up another platform that was wider than the one before and had two ropes hanging down. He gestured for me to go up to join him. With a last look at Betty, who was grinning at me, I followed orders and climbed up to the platform. When I got there, Skip had already put on the harness and was attached to the rope. He instructed me to put on the other harness and attach myself to the other rope.

(Readers, I wish to say at this point that I have no real idea how to rappel. I also have no idea what rappelling equipment is called. However, for the sake of this story, I am pretending I know exactly what I am talking about and request you to pretend along with me.)

Back to it……

Skip leaned out from the platform and stepped off. There he was hanging to his ring thingy with his other hand on the rope, and he told me to do the same thing. *(I have never felt the need to pray, but I did right at that moment and even 'crossed' myself for good measure)* I leaned out and stepped off. 'Slowly does it,' said Skip, 'there is no rush.' My first few inches of rappelling quite went to my head *(yes, I do mean inches!)* I told myself it was easy and then disaster struck. I managed to spin myself around and bumped into Skip, this made him spin too and we managed somehow to spin around each other, ending up face to face. As we looked into each other's eyes, noses nearly pressed together, I could feel a giggle starting, and out it erupted. There we were hanging Lord knows how high above the ground, by now both of us laughing. I had tears in my eyes, and I could feel my nose beginning to run. Suddenly Skip began to unravel us, while still chuckling and I took the opportunity to wipe my nose on my sleeve. Johnny shouted, 'Are you both ok? 'We are fine Sir,' Skip replied, 'we are about to try again.'

Once more we started to rappel, but unfortunately, I was slower than Skip and, in my hurry to catch up, I forgot to continue holding the rope and found myself dangling sort of sideways. I heard a gasp from Betty and Skip shouted at me to place both hands on my hanging thingy and pull myself back upright. This was a bit of a struggle, but I eventually managed to do it. I quickly put my hand back on the rope and started to lower myself again. After what seemed like hours, I eventually made it down to the ground.

'Right,' said Johnny, up you go again. This time you must step off first and Skip will follow you down. Wasn't very easy climbing back up wearing a harness and a hanging down thingy, but I made it. We did this several times until Skip said I was ready to go on my own. I asked for a drink of water as I was by now sweating profusely (*or should that be glowing*?) I drank the water and saying to myself, 'Once more into the breach dear friends' I started climbing up to the platform again.

When I reached the platform, I hooked myself to the rope, and, with ring in one hand and rope in the other, I leaned forward, stepped off and rappelled very carefully all the way to the ground.

Skip slapped me on the back and said, 'Well done, now for the climbing of the ladder.' Skip obviously didn't know his own strength as I found myself running forward, trying not to stumble. After apologising, he led me over to the area where the ladder was hanging. It was 12 inches off the floor. 'Piece of cake.' I said to myself. However, Johnny went to a switch on the wall, turned it on and the ladder began to sway. Betty came up to me and said you will need to put on the harness next to the ladder. As you can see, it is attached to the platform next to the ladder. I will be waiting up there and should you fall off, I will immediately start the motor that will wind you up to the platform. She added that I could do it and suggested I do not look down.

Johnny and Skip wished me luck. I approached the ladder which was by now swinging about merrily. I looked up to check that Betty was on the platform and saw her peering down at me. She gave me the thumbs up sign and, with encouragement from Johnny and Skip, I grabbed the ladder tightly and put my foot on the bottom rung. When my other foot left the floor, I swung crazily backwards and forwards. I was determined not to make a fool of myself this time, so I put my foot back down and tried to steady the ladder. Counting to three, I lifted my foot and placed it on the second rung and so on. I found it easier to go as fast as I could and ignore the nauseous feeling in my stomach. I reached the platform and clambered on it. Betty had been watching me and congratulated me on my speed. Unfortunately, I had to go back down and climb the ladder again. When I was halfway up, Johnny shouted, 'Let go of the ladder.' It took me a couple of seconds to respond but let go I did. I heard the whirring of an engine and felt the harness tighten around me. I could feel myself being drawn upwards, but every now and then the ladder decided to behave like a whip and wacked me hard on any part of my body it could reach. I tried to avoid the ladder by ducking and found myself suddenly hanging upside down. I struggled to turn myself up the right way, to no avail. The relief when I came level with the platform and Betty stopped the engine and assisted me to get the right way up was unbelievable. 'Betty,' I declared, 'I never want to go through that again.' Betty laughed, telling me I was very red in the face. I was beginning to relax when I heard Johnny call for me to come down and repeat the last action again. 'You can go off people you know!' I shouted, climbing down from the platform. Johnny explained I would need to do it until I got the hang of not hanging around the wrong way up. Begrudgingly I went over to the ladder and put one foot on the first rung. Skip turned the switch on again and the ladder twisted and turned. I hung on grimly awaiting the order to let go. This time when the order came to let go, I was prepared for the harness to tighten. I wrapped my arms around the rope to the harness, determined to hang on. Soon I reached the platform and Betty helped me unhitch the harness and climb onto the platform again. 'Well done.' she said.

When we had climbed down to the floor, Betty asked if I would like to try zip lining. We have an activity course nearby, and perhaps we could let off a bit of steam. It's scary, but fun. 'Lead on,' I replied, we can work up an appetite at least.

Betty asked if Johnny and Skip wanted to join us, and after a quick discussion, they decided they would. Johnny said he hadn't been on it for a long time. We left the building after handing in our passes and headed towards a wooded area I hadn't noticed before. It was a treetop course which looked very high to me. It was decided Johnny would go first, followed by Betty, then me, with Skip bringing up the rear.

Chapter 18

Hup High Among the Treetops

'What have I let myself in for? I have spent the whole afternoon going up and down ladders, hanging off platforms and being unceremoniously hauled up in the air at the end of a rope.

There were several ropes hanging down with harnesses on one end and stout clips on the other. We all took one and put on the harness. After a bit of alteration. we were ready to go. I was assured this was a safe course if I made sure I was always clipped to the safety wires. Nodding in confirmation, I watched as Johnny cried 'Geronimo' and started up the ladder. When he reached the platform at the top Betty took her turn. 'See you up there.' She said, 'you are going to enjoy this, honestly!'

When Betty was nearing the top Skip reminded me to attach my harness to the safety wire and sent me on my way. I hooked myself on to the safety immediately I arrived at the platform. Johnny and Betty both smiled at me and, before Skip arrived, Johnny set off on the first challenge. This involved jumping onto a lower platform that was really a trampoline. I had to smile as he rose, before once again landing, but this time he managed to ground himself before standing on a wire that led to the next platform. He reached up and held on to another wire above his head. Taking sideway steps he headed towards the platform.

By now Skip had arrived and Betty jumped down onto the trampoline. Up she came, down she went. She too managed to ground herself and as she saw Johnny step onto the net platform, she set off herself. 'Oh, my word,' I said to Skip, 'It's my turn now.' Skip reassured me, telling me I was going to have a great time. He nudged me and said it was my turn to go. Without taking time to think, I launched myself towards the trampoline. I hit it in the middle and immediately found myself heading back up. Skip gave me the thumbs up sign as I once again fell towards the trampoline. I had every intention of trying to ground like the others had. Unfortunately, I landed on my posterior and with legs akimbo and arms waving, up I went again. On the next down I managed to land flat on my feet, but unfortunately close to the edge and one leg went down into the gap between the trampoline itself and the ring to which it was attached. There I was, sitting with one leg folded under my chin and the other hanging down. No matter how hard I tried, I couldn't get up. I could hear Johnny (who had returned to the first platform with Betty) and Betty laughing and shouting things like – Too early to take a rest and now you've gone and put your foot in it! I looked up and I am ashamed to say I gave them a rather rude sign, which made them laugh even more. I couldn't help but join in because I really was in a ridiculous position.

I looked over my shoulder towards Skip who was rappelling down a rope, landing softly on the trampoline. He asked if I was hurt and when I answered 'only my pride' he carefully walked across it. It was more a skip than a step, which somehow seemed even funnier and set me off laughing again.

Skip was still standing over me, looking a bit concerned. 'Let's hope I can get you out by myself.' he said, bending down to grab me under my arms. I asked him to please be careful not to jump too much because the way I was - umm- sitting, was rather painful. On the count of three, he lifted me, while at the same time I pushed with the bent leg that has been under my chin. As he pulled me, he fell on his back, and I landed atop him. (*Now, can I just say that it was one of the most enjoyable experiences I had ever had, such a pity he was a married man.*)

At the sound of jeering from above, I quickly rolled off him and we both struggled to get up. Skip got up, I attempted to too, causing Skip to fall, which in turn caused me to fall back. Skip instructed me to stay where I was and he would go to the edge of the trampoline and then I should be able to also get up. I promise you I tried, but it was hopeless, so I settled for crawling towards the edge. When I reached it, I managed to get up by holding on to the net at the edge. 'This is where we start climbing again.' said Skip and he started off immediately. I found myself trying to beat him to the top and onto the platform with the others.

When we were all on the platform it became rather crowded, so, after checking I was ok, Johnny set off again to the next platform. It was only when I heard a loud clipping sound and I turned towards it, did I see this time we had to ride a bicycle with no tyres across a line. It had stabilisers at the back of the bike that ran along a wire either side. With a quick wave Johnny set off and when he was halfway across, another bike appeared from below us and Betty climbed on. 'Remember to just look straight ahead!' she called as she pedalled off. Once again, another bike appeared. 'On you get,' Skip instructed, 'remember to look forward, not down, and don't rush, pedal steadily.' Having checked I had my safety clipped on he gave me a gentle push, setting me on my way.

At first, I could feel my heart beating rapidly and telling myself not to be so silly, I started to pedal. It was rather enjoyable and although we were high up, I was still surrounded by trees. I began to take deep breaths and was sorry to reach to end. Betty was waiting for me and reached out to help me off the bike and onto the platform. 'That was brilliant,' I said, 'I do hope there are more exciting things like that.' She told me I would have to wait and see.

I hooked myself on to the safety line and prepared myself for the next experience. We climbed another ladder and onto a further platform. We both hooked ourselves onto the safety wire and climbed aboard a hanging chair, like the type found on ski slopes. Betty pulled a bar across our laps, then pulled a lever on the side of the seat and we set off. We were by now above the treetops and the view was stunning. I could see for miles. There were miles of countryside, with fields that looked like patchwork. I could also see a few houses in the distance and Betty told me it was probably Littlebighampton on the Marsh. All the rich folk lived there and one of the houses was owned by the Pop Star 'Dynamite Dan'. Have you heard of him, he has had several number one hits such as Blow Up My Mind, Love Explosion and not to forget his latest, Let's Get Banging Together. Betty started to sing the last song, it went,

It's time for us to beat the drum, let's awake the dead

People who sleep soundly should waken from their bed

While they sleep the world is gradually falling apart

Waking them up early would enable restitution to start

Let's get banging together, Let's get banging together

'Stop, stop!' I cried, 'that is awful.' 'I know,' she said, 'but he is making millions out of it. Would you like to hear the second verse?' 'NO thank you.' I replied, 'I've heard more than enough.

Meanwhile we had been gathering speed, not g-force, but extremely fast. It was really invigorating, and I found myself laughing out loud. We had been going downwards, but we levelled out, and then started to climb again. I looked across at Betty and she was looking at me and grinning. 'Wait for it,' she said. And as the words left her lips, the chair started to level out once again. We went in a straight line and once more headed down, but even more sharply. Looking ahead I could see Johnny standing on the next platform. We came to a sudden stop, and Betty pushed the safety bar forward and gestured for me to step out. I unclipped and reclipped on the next safety line.

Johnny asked if I was enjoying myself, and, of course, I said I was. He told me this was the last platform and we would now be travelling back to the ground on a zip wire. He pointed out that we would sit astride hanging round wooden seats with a belt that held us in place, hold onto the wooden bar and zip all the way down to the bottom. What he didn't tell me was that the zip wire didn't go straight down, it had many twists and turns and as one went round a corner the seat swung outwards. I followed both of Johnny and Betty down and I could hear Betty screaming and laughing in front of me. I didn't know why until I saw the first corner zooming towards me. Out I swung, or should that swinged, and I too started to scream. I must say, it was something I would not want to have missed for all the pink coloured Smarties in the world.

It wasn't long before we were all at the bottom of the Tree Top experience. We stood around chatting and laughing, especially at me getting stuck in the trampoline. It wasn't over though, the course finished quite a way from the compound.

Chapter 19

Johnny went to a locked shed, pulled out a key to unlock the door and revealed Segway's. These were e-scooters with two wheels side to side and platforms for our feet each side of the pole which led to the handle. Johnny brought one out of the shed and showed me where to turn the Segway on. He stepped onto the feet places and slowly pushed the handlebar forward. It started to roll forward. He then slowly turned to the left, leaning slightly as he did so, and rolled back towards us. 'Your turn.' he said, holding the Segway in front of me. He explained he had it on its lowest speed and not to be afraid of it. 'Here goes nothing.' I thought standing on the Segway and slowly pushed the handle forward. I began to move forward, after about five yards I decided to try to turn around. Turning the handle to the left and leaning slightly I rolled round. Unfortunately, I rolled round further than I wanted and turned a full circle. I could hear Johnny calling out instructions, but, somehow, I was set into circle motion and spun (or should that be span) around again. As I was about to spin for the third time, Johnny grabbed hold of the handle and pulled it up straight. It stopped!

I noticed that once again I was the cause hilarity to the others. I heard things like 'spinning top, disappearing up her own @rse, etc.

'Let's try again,' Johnny said, sniggering, 'take a wider turn, then hopefully you will have time to straighten up.' On I got again, to catcalls. I leant the handle forward gently and moved forward. I went a bit further before I tried turning again. This time I only turned it gently to the left and made a bigger circle, straightening up and heading back to the start to applause from the others.

When everyone had a Segway, Johnny led the way along a sandy pathway. We went in the same order, Betty followed Johnny then me and Skip brought up the rear. (*I found myself thinking how grateful I am that my bum is not huge with lumps and bumps spilling out from my kernickers.*) All went well at first until Johnny suggested we turned up the speed a bit. I had to stop to do that, whereas the others could do it while still riding. Skip overtook me and I turned the speed knob up. Climbed back on my untrusty steed (*I had still not forgiven it for spinning me around like an idiot.*) pushed the handle forward and shot off at what felt like ninety miles an hour. I soon caught up with Skip and overtook him rather dangerously and moved on to catch up with Betty, who heard me coming and quickly moved out of my way. 'Go girl.' she shouted as I hurtled past. Unfortunately, as I headed towards Johnny, he was going round a corner, I panicked, and headed straight on into the bushes bordering the path. I let go of the handle and flew further in and landed in a bed of stinging nettles. At first, I felt nothing, just a bit winded, but then it struck, that awful pins and needles pain in my hands that nettles give you. Johnny came crashing through the hedge and lifted me up. Having checked I wasn't seriously injured, he started to smirk, the smirk changed into a grin and the grin changed into roaring laughter. There I stood, surrounded by stinging nettles, flames licking at my hands (*I know that's an exaggeration, but I am taking a bit of poetic licence here.*) and this arrogant man was laughing at me. I really don't know what happened, but I saw red, and pulled him towards me and then stepped out of the way so he fell into the nettles.

Meanwhile Betty and Skip had rescued my Segway and were leaning in to look at what was going on. At that point Johnny was just landing and hollering. My turn to smirk I thought, as I heard a loud 'Oops' leave my mouth.

Betty realised at once what had happened. She looked from me to Johnny, back at me, then Johnny. I watched a large grin appear on her face, which she swiftly covered with her hand. Skip managed to turn a laugh into a cough, which I thought was very well done. I would tell you what Johnny was saying, but some of the words I couldn't begin to know how to spell, as he was swearing in several different languages. I also caught some of those words that were used here, and yes, those I do know how to spell. My hands were still burning and as Johnny stood, he held his hands away from him. I could see a hives rash appearing, beginning at his hands, and working up the inside of his arms. I nervously looked him in the face and started to splutter apologies. Stopping when I realised it had turned into a stand-off situation with both of us staring at each other. Our two bystanders were busy trying to look sympathetic while at the same time holding in their laughter.

'What are you two staring at?' Johnny demanded adding, 'take hold of her Segway and take it back to the path.' This order was promptly followed through, although I could still hear tamped down laughing from them.

By now I had all sorts of thoughts passing through my head -

I was going to be sent home (without any supper)

I was going to be locked up for the night

I was going to have to face a tribunal

I was going to be Court Marshalled, which is stupid as I don't belong in any of the armed forces

Johnny spoke during my machinations to say, 'Well, seems we are both suffering, so I suggest we head back to camp as soon as possible so we can take Antihistamine. tablets and dab calamine lotion on our stings. 'I really am truly sorry,' I said, 'don't know what came over me!' (*Of course, I knew what came over me, I was reacting to the smug look on his face.*) I have a good idea,' he replied, but as we are both suffering from this little escapade, I think we should shake our hot stinging hands and call a truce!' I was more than happy to do this and held out my and shook his.

Chapter 20

We went back to the path where we found the others still trying to control their laughter, albeit quietly. 'If word gets out on the base, I shall know who the perpetrators are and will give you all the rotten jobs for the next few months. 'Yes Sir.' They replied in unison, looking everywhere but at each other. I had to grin at the pair of them, but they avoided my eyes too.

It was a very chastened group that climbed on their segways and headed towards Base one by one. Nobody spoke or looked at each other until, suddenly out of the blue, Johnny burst into loud laughter. 'I believe I deserved to land in the bed of stinging nettles 'he stuttered between laughs, 'I had forgotten how inexperienced you are.' 'Apology accepted.' I called out to him.

It wasn't long before the start of the umm treetop experience was reached. We alighted from our segways and again they were put inside a lockable shed. We started to chatter away happily, despite the nettle stings, which were calming down by now, we headed towards the vending machine just inside the building and helped ourselves to bottles of water. Johnny then sent for the car and when it arrived, and we all climbed in.

When we were back at the Base, we parted company. I intended to take a long soak in the bath. Johnny promised to send ointment over for my hands as soon as he could.

I started to run a bath and made myself a cup of tea while waiting for the bath to fill up. It wasn't long before the ointment was delivered. I checked on my bath, turned off the taps and got undressed. I gratefully climbed into the water breathing a sigh of happiness. I must have fallen asleep and when I awoke, the water was cold. Smiling to myself I quickly climbed out of the bath, dried myself and got dressed.

I brushed my hair and applied a bit of make-up. Even though they were no longer as painful, I rubbed a bit of ointment into my hands, which took away the rest of the pain. After checking the time, I headed towards the canteen for my evening meal.

I found Betty sitting at the table that seemed to be ours now as nobody else ever sat there. She asked about my hands and then we chatted about the day while deciding what to have to eat. We were pleased to see it was Goldie who was on duty tonight. 'Are yer ready t' order?' she asked smiling at us, making a note of our choices, and promising to be back soon.

I took the opportunity to ask Betty about the next day. She told me we would be heading out early to go to a base some miles away. There was going to be a run through of all I had learned so far, an exercise so to speak and then, if I was happy to continue, I would be given further training. She explained we would be away from Base for several days. The new exercises would be carried out in the Drone. Get tomorrow over and I would be invited to another meeting, after which I would be given a few days off. She suggested I return home and as soon as plans are set, she would phone me, and we could talk everything over.

Goldie brought our meals and confided that she and Ben were getting on so well, he had invited her to go with him to meet his parents. 'You cudda blown me down wiv a feaver,' she said, 'we are gonna take a few days off so I can get to know 'is parents and they me.' We were both so pleased for her and I couldn't help but get up and give her a quick hug. As I said to Betty later, I did notice she had toned herself down and bit and I hoped she wouldn't change too much, or she wouldn't be the woman Ben fell in love with. Just then Johnny and Skip came into the canteen and sat at a table next to ours. After greeting us they looked at the menu. Goldie came to take their orders, and, after a bit of bantering, she made a note of their choice and went back to the kitchen area. While she was gone Johnny and Skip pushed our two tables together and invited us to a sort of nightclub called Bopping in Wopping, which was about a 30-minute drive away from Base. I was confused, what was a sort of nightclub, and was the nightclub called Bopping in wopping or was it just called Bopping and was situated in Wopping? Johnny laughed and told me it was called The Bopping. The town it was in was called Woppery-Underline, but it has always been known as Wopping. He further explained that it is a sort of a nightclub because it was a club and was only open at night. It was more a disco really with a decent bar. Betty and I both agreed to go to the sort of nightclub, saying it would make a nice change. (*Little did we know!*)

Goldie came back with our food. She expertly placed our plates before us saying, 'Two specials wiv chips, enjoy yer meals.' 'Be right back wiv yours.' She said to Johnny and Skip and headed back to the kitchen. Johnny told us to go ahead and eat, as they would soon catch up with us. Back came Goldie with a very heavily laden tray. Skip stood and took it from her so she could place the plates on the table. They had ordered man sized roast beef and vegetables and their plates were almost overflowing. I had no idea how they were going to eat it all, but they soon tucked in and demolished it.

Betty and I had ordered a Crème Brule each, which Goldie brought out to us, but we couldn't believe hearing Johnny order Jam Rolypoly and Skip choosing Treacle Suet Pudding with Custard. 'You must both have hollow legs.' I remarked. These were duly delivered by Goldie, who left to serve others after wishing us an enjoyable time at The Bopping.

Chapter 21

After our meal we left to go back to our rooms. It was decided we would all meet at the front gate at 9pm as the sort of nightclub didn't come alive any earlier than that. Unlocking my door, I was pleased I had packed a decent 'going out dress' and high heeled shoes just in case. Betty was going to call for me as my accommodation was the nearest to the front gate. As it was now gone eight o'clock I didn't waste time getting ready. I redid my makeup and slipped on my 'going out dress.' I was pleased I hadn't gained weight from all the good food I had eaten, but guessed it was all the exercising I was doing that had stopped that happening. It did cross my mind that I should really be having an early night considering the full day I would be having tomorrow, but quickly dismissed it. Tomorrow could take care of itself.

Betty arrived about 8.45pm looking rather grand in a tight-fitting calf length red dress. 'Is that new?' I asked her, 'you look stunning my friend.' 'What? This old thing,' she answered, I have had it for a couple of years and have only worn it once. It's rather tight across the bust, 'she added, 'But I say, if you have it, flaunt it!' I had to agree with her, she certainly had 'it.' Betty pulled a small bottle out of her bag and poured the contents into two glasses she also got out of her bag. She passed one to me. 'Cheers,' she said, and we clinked our glasses together and took a sip. We smiled at each other 'Here's to bopping our bobby socks off tonight.' I added. We took another sip. 'Here's to bopping in Wopping.' Another sip. 'Here's to bopping in Wopping with a lolloping big man.' Betty continued, with another clink of glasses and a sip. 'Here's to bopping without stopping in Wopping.' Said I.

Luckily, there was a knock at the door, which made us both jump, as I feel we were close to hysteria. 'Come in.' I called and Johnny and Skip stepped into the room. Johnny told us they could hear our laughter from outside and said they had decided to see what was causing it.

Meanwhile, Betty and I stood with our mouths wide open. Both Johnny and Skip were dressed like people out of Saturday Night Fever. They looked gorgeous. Closing my mouth with a snap, I opened it again to say, 'What a pair of handsome devils you are. Is this the normal attire for The Bopping?' As one, they bowed before us, admiring our dresses and said it was time to leave. Grabbing my coat and bag we followed them out the door. Johnny locked it for me and led us to a black Staff Car. The driver was holding the rear door open, and we climbed in and settled ourselves. Betty and I facing the front while the two 'John Travolta's' sat facing us. We were quiet on the journey, and I was busy trying to see the buildings etc we were passing, as I had not been this way before. The car started to slow down, and I caught sight of a signpost with an arrow to Woppery-Under-Line. It was by now just five miles away.

We arrived! (*I am going to take time out to describe a bit of The Botting to you.*)

There were a few steps up to the entrance, with double doors that were guarded by two men wearing a sort of suit of armour which seemed to be made of some sort of material, dark glasses like the ones you wear to protect your eyes when drilling a hole for example. They looked more like swimming goggles though. Around their neck chains were hung, which clanked every time they moved. (*By now, my mouth couldn't have fallen open any further.*) Looking upwards I could see the neon sign,' The

Bopping Nigh Club.' It was flashing on and off – almost mesmerising. Sadly the 'T' was missing.

The door opened and a group of people came out, singing 'Agadoodoodoo, shake your nuts in time with me.' (*I know those aren't the right words but they sang them anyway.*) The women were wearing grass skirts and the men had very bright Hawaii shirts on. They continued down the road singing at the top of their voices and pushing each other.

I let a hand come under my chin pushing my mouth shut. I turned to see my three friends laughing at me. 'Are you sure we should go in there?' I asked laughingly, 'I feel very overdressed.' Smiling, they started up the steps, followed by an amazed me. When we reached the umm – armoured doormen, Johnny greeted them. 'Good evening Galla, good evening Merle, you both well?' I looked towards Betty in askance who said, 'Galla Goodman and Merle Merryman. I quickly turned a laugh into a cough, he didn't look very merry...

In the foyer was an old-fashioned kiosk with an aging lady in charge. Johnny walked up to it and asked for four tickets. As I watched she tore out four raffle tickets and handed them to him. 'That'll be twenty pounds please.' she said holding out her hand. The raffle prize tonight is a fruit basket.' Johnny thanked her and gave her a twenty-pound note. I pinched myself to make sure I wasn't dreaming – a fruit basket raffle prize in a Night Club?

'Come on,' Johnny called, 'time to experience Bopping Wopping style. He led us to the door into the nightclub. The music was very loud. I didn't recognise it but I could feel my body begin to sway in time to it. Johnny went up to the bar and asked to open a tab for the four of us. He then asked what we would like to drink. Once more my mouth opened as I looked at the bartender. He was the most handsome man I had ever seen. His face by almost too symmetrical. He had dark brown/almost black eyes, very dark hair which was long and tied back with a band at the nape of his neck. He was also tall and broad shouldered He was busy getting our drinks, so he was either too busy to see me staring or was so used to it he didn't take any notice. Betty again put her hand under my chin and closed my mouth, saying, 'Don't even think about going there.' She looked at the bartender and back at me, 'he is a gigolo, known locally as Troy the Toy-Boy. 'He is kept busy when not working behind the bar, you watch, he will be approached by ladies of a 'certain age' and they will check their diaries and make an umm appointment.'

Betty led me to a tall table with four orange plastic bar stools around it. The table was a bright Florescent green. Quite honestly, I couldn't believe my eyes. I heard Betty laughing and looked at her shaking my head saying, 'If I hadn't seen this with my own eyes, I wouldn't have believed it.' 'Look at the walls she suggested, sort of smirking.

Chapter 22

(Well readers, I am finding it very hard to describe the walls, and the rest of the 'nightclub' but I will do my best.)

The walls had vertical flashing strobe lights that changed colour in time to the beat from the music playing. There were several alcoves that were lit from above and held Greek statues. While I was busy looking at these, Johnny and Skip came to the table with our drinks. 'So,' Johnny asked, 'what do you think of this classy joint?' 'Classy!' I exclaimed, 'it is beyond classy to uniquely unparalleled old drug-inducing gloriously colourful mayhem.' This caused merriment around the table, with the others repeating my words. Johnny even went so far as to say he had never heard a more accurate description.

Just then the music started. I looked towards the DeJay's corner, which once again gave me rather a shock. The Dejay was only about 5 feet tall and had to stand on a box to set up the cd's. He had orange hair that he been permed and looked rather like a large curly wig stuck on his head. He had an earring in one ear with a chain which was hanging beneath his chin and attached to his other ear. He also had a parrot sitting on his shoulder which, at a closer look, was a real dead parrot that had been stuffed. Betty whispered in my ear that the parrot had died a few months ago and he had had it stuffed. The piratical image was completed by an eye patch, which he had to lift to see the next cd, and a pirate's jacket, with trousers tucked into black wellies. Evey now and then he would put a plastic cutlass in his mouth and mumble. 'Avast me hearties or splice the mainbrace. The music was a mixture of Northern soul, Southern Jazz, and Funk, with a spattering of 60' and 70's classics. He had just lined up the next cd and pressed start. We sat to the table and watched the people dancing. There was every age group vying for a good place on the dance floor. It made fascinating watching.

It was the song 'Staying Alive' that caused a mass dash to the dance floor, the Northern Soulers who had been the only ones on the dance floor were abruptly pushed aside by the 60's dancers strutting their stuff. This was followed by Thriller, which got us four up off our seats and dancing on our way to the floor. This was a double length feature cd, and the Dejay, known as 'Flash Harry Heartbreaker' (real name Harold Shortshanks) left his podium (box) and made straight for Betty. He then began making moves known only unto him trying to impress her. As you know, Betty is tall for a woman and Flash Harry's head only came up to her bosom. Suddenly Flash Harry grabbed her and started spinning around. Johnny came closer and told me it happens every time they came here, just wait. Flash Harry suddenly spoke into a microphone he had in his hand. Looking at Betty he said, 'Avast me proud beauty, wanna know why my Roger is so jolly?' followed by, 'I'd love to drop anchor in your lagoon!'

Betty stopped lifted her hand and slapped Flash Harry on the cheek. This brought forth cheers from the other dancers. A red-faced Flash Harry turned to the other dancers saying, 'Time to weigh anchor and hoist the Mizzen!' and on this note he slunk back to his podium (box).

After this bit of excitement, while I was still moving to the music I glanced across to where Troy was serving drinks. A woman wearing dark glasses walked towards the bar with her arms held out in front of her. I noticed she went to the other end of the bar and stood waiting. Troy finished serving the drinks, took the money and then casually strolled to the woman with a smile on his face. They spoke quietly and I watched Troy pull a small notebook/diary from his bartender's apron. The woman withdrew a diary from her bag. She quickly looked around to ensure nobody was close and watching. She and Troy walked a little more, he nodded, and they both made a note in their respective diaries. 'That's Sherie Shorestart,' Betty whispered my ear, 'she thinks nobody recognises her behind those sunglasses, but everyone knows who she is and that she is a member of the Desperate Danglers that come in here. There's quite a few of them, many of whom have husbands that go to sea for long periods at a time.

We smiled at each other and carried on dancing. 'Oh, look out, here comes Milly Ditherah

.She is heading straight towards Troy. Let's dance over that way so we can hear them, I think you will enjoy the conversation. It went like this:

Troy: Good Evening, Milly, nice to see you.

Milly: H h hello Troy (and she stood there staring at him.)

Troy: Would you like the usual day?

Milly: Oh, yes, no, umm -I think so.

Troy: Wednesday afternoon?

Milly: Yes, no, yes, but later if you can. I have visitors coming in the afternoon. Perhaps I should change it to Thursday.

Troy: (After looking in his book which I now saw was red) I can't do Thursday afternoon, but I could perhaps slip in in the morning.

Milly: Oh no, that won't do, I am having my hair done at ten and I wouldn't want it mussed up. Perhaps Wednesday morning about elevenish, no, make that tennish.

Troy: Can't do Wednesday morning, how about Friday, I am free in the afternoon.

Milly: Oh yes, oh no, damn, it's Jerusalem and Jam afternoon and there is going to be a talk on the mating habits of Squirrels by Reverand St John Cocksure with slides.

Troy: (Now sounding just a little impatient) So how about we leave it until next week, normal day, normal time?

Milly: But I really wanted to show you, my melons. I have grown them from seeds, and I am hoping to get a prize for them at the Nuns Garden Show in a couple of weeks.

(I turned to Betty and asked if I had heard that right, 'The Nuns Garden Show?' Betty nodded, the Nuns from Saint Diggers Nunnery hold this every year to raise funds for improvements to the Nunnery and anything else they need. I went once, it was an insipid affair, all we had to drink was homemade lemonade or homemade beer. I'll tell you more later)

Troy: Why don't I pop in quickly early Wednesday evening to view your melons?

Milly: (Sounding very excited) What a good idea, I haven't shown my melons to anyone, but you.

Has Connie Cantelope shown you, her melons?

Troy: Actually, she has, they are coming on nicely. Her husband, Charlie, has the biggest onions I have ever seen, and his corn-on-the-cob will be ready for plucking.

Milly: I thought Charlie was into Brassicas. Last year his purple sprouting broccoli was way ahead of anyone else's. However, his cucumber was a great disappointment.

         (By now I was close to screaming with laughter, as was Betty. Troy looked across at us and winked. That was us finished, we quickly ran to the Ladies rest room, collapsing onto a couple of chairs.

Me: 'Talk on the mating habits of squirrels.'

Betty: 'Have you seen Connie's melons?'

Me: `   'Quick, let's go order another round of drinks, I don't want to miss anything.'

         Troy knew why we were there and called he only be a few minutes.

Milly: Right, you will pop in to see my melons and yes, I would like to book for next Wednesday at the normal time.

Troy: Yes, next Wednesday booked and I will pop in to see your melons as promised.

         (As he said that, he looked at us and winked again.)

Milly: Thank you Troy, see you then.

Troy: You will, I do enjoy viewing melons.

After their goodbyes, Troy came to us and took our repeat order. 'I don't suppose you have any melons you would like to show me?' he asked. 'Not on your life,' Betty replied, 'my melons are staying right where they are.' Giggling, we turned towards our table, 'Good luck with Milly's melons.' I called. Laughing, Troy waved us on our way as we headed back to our table. Skip was still dancing but Johnny was back. Smiling in greeting he asked if we were having a good time. We told him about Troy and his conversation with Milly. Laughing, he told us that Molly only bought his company, nothing else. He sits with her for a couple of hours and a chat. He also did little things for her like painting her bathroom and mending her fence. He has become the son she never had. I said that I had thought so, she is such a sweet little lady.

I then asked if Connie Cantelope was there this evening. Looking around, Johnny pointed out a woman who was in the dance floor. Mutton dressed as lamb came to mind. She had long bleached blond hair with red tips. It also looked as though she had had a facelift (or two) because she looked permanently surprised. False eyelashes fluttered like fans, and she was dressed in a silver jump suit with no sleeves and a rather low frontage. High heeled silver sandals completed the unusual ensemble. Suddenly Skip appeared at the table, all hot and bothered. He had asked a woman for a dance, she accepted and proceeded to flirt with him. 'We were just dancing,' he said, 'when this man came over and stood between us and threatened to punch my lights out.' He was her husband, so I beat a hasty retreat.

There was a bit of argy-bargy going on in the dance floor. The couple were shouting at each other, and a circle was forming around them. Flash Harry changed the CD to 'The Eye of the Tiger' which made us laugh. I noticed he was standing on his podium (box) and shouting 'fight, fight, fight through his microphone. To my surprise, the woman socked her husband on the chin with an amazing right-handed hook. This shook him a little and he started roaring at her. 'You wait 'til I get you home, I am going to confiscate your credit cards for a start.' Her prompt reply 'I've got no credit left on them anyway!' This brought a loud cheer of approval from the other women and a groan from the men. Someone needled him and enraged, he turned to punch the man. That seemed to have triggered a free for all and all we could hear was swearing, a slapping noise from the punches and screaming. There was also a lot of hair pulling and name calling by the women.

Johnny suggested we drink up and leave before the husband remembers who his wife was dancing with. We quickly complied while Johnny went to pay our tab. On his return we grabbed our handbags and with Johnny in front and Skip at the rear we slunk out single file. We stopped at the kiosk to get our coats and the woman offered to keep our tickets in case we won the fruit basket. While betty and I thanked her, Johnny called the staff car to come and collect us. We all got in as quickly as we could because the noise from the nightclub was getting louder and louder, which meant they were all being hustled out by Gallahad and Merle. A quick decision was made to head back to camp, especially as we had a full day tomorrow. When we arrived, they walked me to my door and I thanked them for an exciting and interesting evening and, fishing the key out of my bag, I unlocked my door. Before entering I turned to watch my three comrades walking towards their quarters. Betty's laugh carried to me on the wind, and I wondered which part of the evening she was chuckling about. Yawning, I entered my room, went straight to the bathroom to remove my makeup, clean my teeth, and get undressed ready for bed. I found myself laughing at the odd things that had happened. I set my alarm, climbed into bed, and promptly fell asleep.

Chapter 23

Suddenly I found myself back at the Nightclub and Flash Harry was on the dance floor next to me, talking his stupid pirate phrases and whacking me with his dead parrot. I tried to escape him, but the crowd had formed a circle and were cheering him on. Every time his parrot hit me, feathers flew everywhere, and the crowd cheered 'she's been feathered!' I called for help and caught sight of Troy Toyboy who was cheering along with the rest of them. Searching in my bag for my phone to call for help I found my bag was full of Brussel sprouts. I decided to use them as weapons and started to throw them at Flash Harry and members of the crowd that were getting too close for comfort. To my surprise, when they hit their target, the sprouts exploded. 'This is more like it.' I thought taking aim at the people who had just jeered. I heard several 'fffft bangs' following by cries of pain. People began to move back, but I was still lobbing sprouts at anyone I could. Flash Harry was now on his knees begging me to stop. 'I think not,' I thought, 'You are a pain in the proverbial and deserve to be sprouted. Sprouted I thought to myself, I shall never complain about them ever again.

Most of the people who had stood around me jeering had now fallen back. I noticed one or two of them had burn marks in their clothes, and one had smouldering hair.

I soon ran out of sprouts, and before the crowd realised this I cried out 'TallyHo' and a pack of dogs entered the dance floor followed by Johnny, Betty and Skip all sitting on one horse. Galloping the horse over to me, Johnny leaned down and grabbed my arm, instructing me to climb on soonest. Doing what I was told, I almost flew up on the back of the horse then flew straight off the other side. Johnny grabbed me again and up I flew, this time I stayed, but facing the wrong way. Somehow the horse had expanded to give me room to sit. Skip started to speak to me in a native American tongue. He was offering me words of comfort and what the plan was to aid my escape. All I heard was, 'Tiki Awowa! followed by 'Me aarwen whooshup Kemosabe.' As I did not know what that meant, I took it to mean, 'We are here to save you.' Betty suddenly started making a noise that was a cross between yodelling and yelping. She had a spear in her hand with feathers stuck out the back. Johnny then produced a tomahawk. I put my hand in my pocket and withdrew an old-fashioned American handgun. I had no idea where that came from as I had never been to America. However, being careful not to shoot anybody else on the horse I took aim and fired. A flag appeared from the barrel of the gun with BANG written on it. Despite that, one of the usprouted ones suddenly jerked and fell to the floor. I quickly shoved the bang back in and aimed at another person, pulled the trigger and 'banged, another person, who also fell. Meanwhile Johnny was throwing his tomahawk hitting people in the back, after they fell, he retrieved it ready to throw it again. The dogs were barking in a threatening manner, nipping people's rear ends. Suddenly I felt Betty's spear whoosh by my head just as she started chanting, 'On the shores of Gitche Gumee.' I was listening to her, while watching Skip, who had somehow produced and bow and arrow, which he was busy firing as fast as he could. I stopped him from going further and shouted 'Ceasefire' and then bang, I awoke! But immediately fell back asleep.

The ringing of my alarm woke me the next morning. My dream promptly entered my head, or was it a dream? It felt so real. I lay thinking about it for a few minutes. 'I hope the dogs are ok.' I said to myself. The phone rang, it was Betty to say there was no rush, have a good breakfast and we are to meet up in the canteen at 11.00am. She also suggested I wear the flying suit she was going to send over in a few minutes. She laughed and told me it was going to be an exciting day and she was sure I would do very well.

Having taken another quick bath, I phoned over to the canteen for a toasted bacon sandwich and a pot of tea, which arrived ten minutes later. As did the flying suit. It was navy blue and very smart of course. At 10.50am I strolled over to the canteen. Johnny, Betty, and Skip were waiting just inside the door. I saw the staff car parked outside and after 'Good Mornings' all-round Johnny herded us towards the vehicle. Johnny asked how I was feeling, and I replied that I was feeling good but a little apprehensive and I was looking forward to today.

Chapter 24

We were driven to the secret test site, and I could feel tension in the car. Nobody spoke, we all spent the journey looking out the windows of the car.

We passed a beautiful old church with a graveyard surrounding it. Some bright spark had made a sign that read 'Dead Centre of Holebury Town. I couldn't help it, I burst out laughing, as did Skip who had seen it too. At least it lightened the feeling inside the car. The next village we drove through was Little Puffington and, of course, it had a miniature train that ran through a miniature village situated in a park.

Finally, we arrived and, once again, there was high security. We were searched and our passes were thoroughly scrutinised. There were several armed guards standing around too. 'Goodness,' I thought, 'there's security and there is SECURITY!' Johnny took us to a lounge area inside the building. I was asked to wait while the others passed through to another room behind a security door. I noticed a guard was on duty, just standing by the door. I smiled at him, but he just frowned back.

About a quarter of an hour later the security door opened and Betty came out. She motioned for me to join her inside the room. I hadn't realised, but this was a small room in the big hanger and in the middle of it sat the biggest Drone I had ever seen. Johnny joined us and motioned to the Drone. As we watched a door opened on the side of the Drone, steps lowered to the floor automatically, and a man dressed in a navy-blue flying suit came down the steps and saluted Johnny and Betty. He then shook Skips hand. Johnny introduced him to me as Senior Airman Rupert Allman. We shook hands and Johnny gestured towards the Drone. We walked towards it and climbed the steps and entered.

Inside was unbelievable. There was a bank of computers which were all flashing. A printer was receiving data and printing it out as it did so. In front of three of the screens we three gaming type chairs. There was also one near the door of the Drone and another next to that. Rupert sat by the door and Johnny gestured to me to put a harness on and sit next to him. Johnny sat at the controls and Betty at the screen collecting data. We all spun so we were facing each other, and Johnny explained the mission for the day.

At first, we were only going to fly, not doing anything as this was just for me to acclimatise to the motion. We would fly in a circle and return. Then the exercise would begin. This is where I came in, The Drone would hover in the air and I would rappel down the rope as quickly as I could, grab the package left there, place it in my backpack, run and grab the rope, put one foot in the loop and hang on for dear life. Meanwhile Rupert would be in control of the rope and would whip me back up as fast, but as carefully as he could. Skip will be waiting at the door to help me in, and we would immediately zoom away and back to base. Everything will be recorded and printed, and we will land for a while to test the computers were recording everything correctly.

The next part of the exercise will involve you being left on the ground, we will once again fly round in a circle, the rope will be lowered and you will need to run grab the rope, hang on while putting your foot in the loop. Hold on as you will be hoisted up very quickly, assisted to get into the Drone. Once you have reached the door, Skip will grab you and the Drone's power will be increased. We will then return to base for a quick lunch and short discussion. If you feel up to it, we will repeat the exercises once more. The records will then be handed to the Boffins who will further analyse the results.

'Right, let's get this show on the road,' Johnny said, 'take your positions. I felt the Drone lift off and we sped off in a circle. It did feel strange I must admit, but not too bad. Johnny was flying it, which surprised me, I don't know why, I thought Rupert would. The Drome stopped and Skip push the button to send the rope down until it trailed on ground. I was then ordered to rappel down the rope to collect the parcel I would find there.

I hooked my harness onto the rope and rappelled to the ground. I could see the package, but it was a bit further away from the rope than I anticipated. Unhooking myself from the rope I ran to it, picked it up and placed it in the special bag on my harness and ran towards the rope, put my foot into the loop. I held on tightly as I felt the rope being wound back up to the Drone. When I reached the door, Skip helped me in and the then Drone sped off. (*I would like to say Warp 5, but that's from a television programme.*) Skip closed the door and helped me off with the harness.

A minute later we arrived back at the base and were looking forward to a bit of lunch. Chatting about the exercise on the way. Johnny said he felt it was successful, but if I was willing, he would like for us to do it again that afternoon. I agreed. I began to feel rather proud of myself, but as we all know, pride comes before a fall!!!

Lunch was a buffet style, the usual things like sausage rolls, quiche, vol-au-vents, crisps, and mixed salad. Tea and coffee were available from flasks. I filled my plate, got a cup of tea, and sat at the table with the others. They were all discussing how the morning had gone and trying to find ways to improve it. I sat and quietly ate my food if you can call crunching crisps quiet. I had two vol-au-vents and thought they tasted a bit strange, but they were rather nice, so I ate them. Johnny apologised that I was left out of the conversation, but I told him I fully understood and to carry on. I knew it was important and was really pleased to just sit and eat after the morning's activity. When we had all finished, Johnny suggested we take a comfort break and meet outside the Drone. Betty and I went into the Ladies together, chatting about nothing much, like how delicious lunch was and how we were still laughing about the Nightclub.

We met up at the Drone and Johnny said we would be repeating the morning's exercise. Rupert pushed a button on a remote control he was holding, and the door of the Drone opened, and the steps came down. Once again, we climbed aboard and sat in our appointed places. Johnny took the controls, and we lifted off. Rupert helped me on with my harness and when the Drone began to hover, he opened the door and lowered the rope. When it reached the ground, I grabbed the rope, attached my harness, and started down as quickly as I could. Unfortunately, halfway down I slipped and lost my hold on the rope. There I was swinging to and fro trying to grab the rope as I passed. Rupert was shouting instructions from above, but the wind had got up and was determined I would not be able to grad the rope. Then Betty called down to me telling me to hang on and they would rewind the rope and bring me back in. She laughed, calling down that I was nothing but a 'flighty woman.' I gave up and just hung about, giggling. Up I went, got level with the door and Rupert told me to take hold of the rope, properly this time, and he would send me back down again. This time hanging on grimly, I made it all the way down to the ground, unhitched my harness, grabbed the package, and shoved it in the bag attached to the harness, ran to catch up with the rope, placed my foot in the loop, feeling the rope being wound upwards. Unfortunately, my foot slipped, and I was now half sitting on the end of the rope while desperately trying to reclip my harness. I could hear Rupert explaining to the others what had happened, while slowly winding me in.

I began to feel rather 'icky' and regretted eating so much for lunch. Suddenly, whoosh, out 'it' came. I vomited up everything I'd had for lunch. By now Rupert was making gagging noises as I had reached the entrance and he 'copped' an eyeful. I felt so bad, as he gallantly pulled me in before wiping his face with a tissue. I wanted the floor to open and swallow me (not a good idea as we were up in the air.) I felt the drone begin to lower to the ground and once more I felt my stomach lurch. I put my hands over my mouth trying to hold it in. Rupert grabbed his hat and held it under my chin. I looked up at him and he was smiling at me. 'I'm so sorry,' I gasped, 'I really don't know what happened. I am not a sicky person.'

Betty brought a bottle of water to take a drink, and with a damp cloth, wiped my face. She gave me a gentle hug too. Rupert had stepped back, saying how glad he was I hadn't taken advantage of his hat offer.

After closing down the engine, Johnny came to see how I was, telling me I looked like I had turned into the Grinch, I was so green about the gills. Skip was reporting back to base to explain what had happened and he was informed that several people who had eaten the chicken vol-au-vents had also been sick. They were being looked after in the sick bay and an ambulance would be sent to pick me up and take me there too. I must admit I was pleased to hear that because I was feeling woozy. It was decided Rupert go with me as the exercise could be carried out with Skip taking my place. The poor man needed to clean up himself. When the ambulance arrived, I was wrapped in a blanket and helped down the steps and into the ambulance. Rupert followed me in and smiled when the paramedic took the micky out of him for smelling of sick and still had some in his hair. 'Thought it was scrambled eggs,' they said,' not chicken vol-au-vents when you rise through the ranks.

It didn't take long to reach the sickbay and Rupert told me the Drone had left. Once again, I apologised, but smiling, he told me not to worry at all.

Chapter 25

I spent the next two days in sick bay together with several others. We became a happy band, comforting each other as we took turns holding our heads over sick bowls. The other sufferers were secretaries and typists who typed up information as it came in. They were sworn to secrecy of course, but despite the importance of their work, they were a cheerful bunch. Their names were Sally Serene, Angie Reddit, Paula Lawler, Barbara Bloomers, and the only fellow, Perri Summerbottom. As in most situations like this we became friends very quickly.

Sally was the serious one, very proper, a lady in every sense of the word, and a Mother Hen.

Angie reads all the time, she always has a book in her hand and cheerfully misquotes Shakespeare, Jane Austen and even Hippocrates. She was a source of delight to us all.

Paula was very athletic, she even exercised between bouts of sickness. Wore me out just watching her, but the others seemed happy to ignore it, so eventually I did too.

Barbara was sex on legs, stunningly beautiful with a bouncy personality. She was always 'Up' never 'Down' no matter what happens. She was prone to using her looks to get what she wanted, but she didn't laud it over the rest of us.

Last, but not least, Perri. What can I say? He fitted in so well with us women, happy to discuss makeup, nails, even going so far as to apply pretty nail varnish for us all. Mine were green with a white daisy flower. Never having worn nail varnish before I couldn't stop looking at them. Of course, Barbara wore red nails varnish with glittery hearts on them. His own nails were rainbows, he had had a friend do them for him before he became ill. He was also exceptionally house-proud, clearing up after us all. All with a smile on his face, bless him.

Rupert came to visit my first evening bearing good wishes from Johnny, Betty, and Skip. They had completed the exercise and were busy uploading their findings. He told me they would be coming to visit the next morning. He stayed and chatted with us all for an hour or so. His visit caused a bit of a stir because they had all admired him from afar, him being high above them in rank. After he left, they tried to find out where we had met, but I couldn't say because I was unsure how top secret my top secret was.

I slept well that night, No silly dreams. In fact, they had to wake me up for breakfast. Not that we were allowed to eat much, dry toast and Barley Water that made me shudder when I drank it. Oh, how I yearned for a cup of tea. I was promised one if I stayed vomit free for the next six hours.

Poor Barbara had been ill in the night, but it was her own fault as she had eaten a bag of chocolate covered raisins. She didn't look her perky self but brightened up when Johnny, Betty and Skip visited me for a while. They all three hugged me, which caused whispering amongst the others. We went into the small garden behind the ward so we could talk privately about the exercises the day before. They now had enough information to present to the man at the top about the suitability of the Drones flown by people could undertake tasks that other forms of transport are unable to. Johnny also said that though it is top secret, as I had taken part in the exercises, I deserved to know that a Stealth Drone was being developed, but it would take a year or so before it can even be tested the same way this one had.

It was amazing how many of the others with food poisoning found reasons to come into the garden. Of course, as to be expected, Barbara was the first. She apologised for disturbing us, but she was picking a few flowers to go on the dining table in the ward to cheer us up. She then pointedly stood by the table awaiting introductions to my colleagues. Smiling to myself, I did so. She promptly sat down and started flirting with the men. When they didn't respond as she wished, she turned to Betty and asked if it was true that she had slapped Flash Harry the other night. Betty nodded and we all laughed at the memory, and Betty explained further to Barbara, who was about to ask another question when Paula came out and started to warm up ready for her run. She stretched her legs and touched her toes. She then did a few arms up to the sky, then wide and then back. Johnny and Skip watched her with enjoyment, until Paula suddenly started to run in circles around the little garden. I began to feel quite dizzy watching her. We all seemed to be mesmerised as she flew past us at one-minute intervals.

Out came Angie, book in hand. She approached us at the table, opened her book at a page showing the Statue of Liberty and asked if any of us had ever been to see it. 'This is Angie,' I said and the person whizzing around us is Paula.' 'How do's.' were exchanged and Skip answered Angie's question in the affirmative. Angie then asked if there were stairs inside or lifts. Skip thought for a while and told her. I used the stairs. They are spiral staircases, one leading up and another leading down. They are narrow, steep, and shallow. The statue is said to be the height of 20 floors. Impressed, Angie asked how he managed to hold all that information and he replied saying that he seemed to have a head for figures. (*Now, of course I didn't know all about the Statue of Liberty, but I checked it out for the sake of this here book.*)

Now the statement that he seemed to have a head for figures set Barbara off again, as she said, 'I do love a man who has a head for figures.' Shaking his head, Skip laughingly shook it off.

It was Sally who came out next, followed by Perri. Sally was carrying bottles of water and Perri had a large plate of biscuits he had 'found' in the nurses' pantry. Once again. I did the introductions. Sally insisted we all drink the water before we ate biscuits. We dutifully did as she asked, including Johnny, Betty, and Skip. I was inwardly laughing at their expressions as I doubted water loomed very large in their choice of liquid. Perri danced around us offering to get tea or coffee to dunk our biscuits in.

Betty shot to her feet, 'Perri, dear boy,' she called, 'what are you doing here?' She hugged him enthusiastically. 'Oh Perry, I have missed you, how are you? Silly question, I can see you are ok, did you get food poisoning too? She asked, at last stopping to breath. Those two worked together a few years ago, they are great friends. We won't get anything out of either of them now.' Johnny mumbled. Perry and Betty were sitting in a bench in the garden talking away.

Angie started to cross examine Skip further on the Status of Liberty. As she remarked, it's one thing to read about it, but much better to talk to someone who has been there. Barbara fell asleep in a hammock she found strung up between two trees. Even asleep she was beautiful, no snoring and dribbling for her, oh no, just a gentle regular breath. Paula stopped running around and went inside for a shower, leaving just Johnny and me.

Johnny reminded me I had some time off for a while. I would be driven home and £2,000 would be paid into to my bank, to be spent as I wished. Betty and I will come and see you in a couple of weeks, we will ring you beforehand, to discuss future offers and exercises. We are all very impressed with the way you handled yourself over the past few weeks. You proved that it is possible to train civilians, especially woman, to cope with that training in a short time. I will certainly miss your company for sure, but hopefully this was not the end, and we would be working together again soon. He thought it only fair I be informed the next mission involved spending time in Switzerland. We need to know how the Drone reacts to intense cold, and then we will be going to Africa to see how it behaves in heat. I told him I would certainly give it some thought while I was back home.

Chapter 26

I had begun to feel homesick, I missed my cat, my own bed, my friends, even though I had phoned home several times a week to check everything was ok. I would have enough money to pay off my credit card and a tidy amount in the bank.

It wasn't long before my three friends took their leave, having insisted we lunch together the next day, so proper goodbyes could be said. I was pleased about this because I had grown fond of the people who helped to run it.

Our evening meal was ready, a table had been laid up in the garden as it was still nice and warm. As we had not eaten properly for a couple of days, and had no further bouts of sickness, we were to be served food guaranteed not to upset our stomachs. Looking at the menu I saw we had Cream of Chicken soup with croutons, followed by Chicken Casserole with herb dumplings and to finish off, Banoffi Pie with ice cream.

I noticed there was an extra place, and just then Rupert arrived. I must admit I was pleased to see him. 'Good evening, everyone,' he said, coming towards me to place a kiss on my cheek. Rupert sat next to me at the table and when the others were chatting, he turned towards me, saying he understood I was going home for a while the day after tomorrow. I confirmed this and he asked to have a quiet word when we could be alone. I nodded my head and then we turned back to join in the general conversation. I did wonder what he wanted to talk about but decided to enjoy this meal with the people who I would probably never see again and who had come to be friends. I must admit I don't remember much about the meal as I was puzzled about what Rupert wanted to discuss.

At the end of the meal, which was full of bantering and laughter, we all helped clear the table and Perri produced a pack of cards from his pocket, and we spent a happy hour playing Chase the Ace. Of course, a lot of cheating went on, cards being passed to each other under the table, which made it more fun. Rupert got up and went to his car, coming back with a couple of bottles of wine. The rest of us surreptitiously crept inside to get our water glasses and somehow an extra glass appeared.

When the first bottle was empty, a game of Spin the Bottle was enacted. Whomever the bottle head pointed to had to pay a forfeit. Of course, it was me first, and everyone got into a huddle after a bit of discussion, I had to juggle three oranges, after stealing them from the kitchen. I had done two- balls before but hadn't graduated to three balls. After my ham-fisted attempt, I knew I could never run away and join the circus as a professional juggler. The more I tried the worse I got, but the jeering and laughter made it worse. Finally, they called a stop luckily and the bottle was spun again. This time it pointed at Perri, and his task was to pretend to be a model and his forfeit was to strut his stuff on a catwalk. He rushed indoors and donned his pink fluffy dressing gown with a hood. Unfortunately, it trailed along the ground, which left us feeling a cross between apprehension and amusement at what could happen.

We all clapped and cheered as he posed at the end of the path. He had the hood up which he dramatically flung back before walking towards us. The nursing staff came out to see what all the noise was about. One of them whistled between her fingers and Perri stopped, hands on his hips, one leg forward and chin held up high, then with a tossing of his head, he carried on walking. When he reached the table, he struck a pose. We all whistled and cheered, totally forgetting we were in the Sick Bay. He turned and began to mince back, placing one foot directly in front of the other in a perfect model walk. Once more he turned and headed back towards us, but this time he had undone his dressing gown and holding it back at his waist with his hands on his hips he revealed a striped grandad bed shirt. It was too much or us, we were laughing so hard we couldn't breathe.

'WHAT THE HELL IS GOING ON HERE? Shouted Matron, 'stop this noise at once, you have woken up the other patients. Now back inside all of you. Thank goodness you are leaving tomorrow. We stood stock still, trying to look sorry until Matron turned and went back inside. Quick thinking Barbara grabbed the full bottle of wine, hiding it beneath her cardigan, she winked and headed back inside. The others quickly joined her, and I walked with Rupert back to the car park still giggling. When we reached the gate, he suddenly blurted out that he had a holiday due too, and asked if we could perhaps share it together. He said he understood I needed to head home and check everything is ok there. He asked, if I thought it would be alright, for him to go with me. He would book into the local pub or something so I wouldn't feel pressured. He added that he had felt very drawn to me and would like to see if it would come to something deeper. He hadn't felt this way about any woman before, and I didn't have to make up my mind now, we could talk further tomorrow. Looking at him I thought of how kind he had been. He wasn't the most handsome man in the world, but there again, I wasn't a great beauty. We did get on well together so I told him I didn't need to wait until tomorrow, I could answer him now. I felt like him and would also like to pursue it. I would appreciate him taking a room in a pub, but not the one where Betty and Johnny stayed in when they came. In fact, a lady across the road, Mrs Clara Carbunkle, who sometimes lets rooms. She is lovely but is getting on a bit. She never had children of her own, so she spoils her visitors as if they were family. She will probably love you to death. I will give her a ring and see if she has a room. If not, I am sure we can find something else. So saying, I sent Rupert off before we got into more trouble with Matron, saying I would see him tomorrow.

Rupert bent down to kiss me on the cheek. Then waving to the others who had crept back outside to watch, clutching glasses full of wine, he called a Goodnight to the ladies and Perri. As you can imagine, they were full of questions. How long have you known him? Is he unmarried? Where does he come from, is he from around here? Are you an item? Where did you meet? I decided it was best to tell the truth where I could and answered their questions in order. I met him yesterday, he's single, no idea where he's from. We might end up an item. Met him on the base. I am heading home day after tomorrow so don't know if we will meet up again. On that note I headed back to sick bay, had a quick shower, put on my nightclothes, and climbed into bed. The rest of the girls soon did the same and before long we were all fast asleep.

Morning came as morning does. I woke wondering why I felt so thirsty, then I remembered what had happened the evening before. I lay in bed thinking about Rupert and felt my heart skip a beat as a big smile crossed my face.

'Hey you! Good morning,' called Barbara, 'we are out of jail today. Word is you're having lunch with your friends later. Would you like me to do your hair and makeup for you?' I realised Barbara was really a very kind woman. (*Isn't it funny how we judge people without really knowing them*) 'Oh,' I replied, I would really love that. I've got packing to do, but, if I am careful, I won't spoil it. 'Come on then,' she said, getting out of bed, gathering her washing things, and headed towards the bathroom. The others were just waking up, so I explained Barbara's offer. Paula told me Barbara had done the same for her a while ago, and how good she had looked. She quickly dressed into her running gear and, after hugging me and saying goodbye, she set off on her morning run. Angie came in, and, to my surprise, she was fully dressed. 'I will say goodbye now,' she said, 'I am off to the library in Woppery Underline. I need a book on Windsor Castle, one full of information. I have booked a trip to Windsor and have a ticket to enter the castle. I've checked out the library on base, but they don't have one with enough detail.' Off she went after a hug and hopes we will meet again. Angie looked very odd with no book in her hand.

Barbara came out of the bathroom and sent me in. I saluted her as I passed, and she saluted me back, grinning. 'Don't be long.' She ordered.

Chapter 27

Let the Makeover Begin

Barbara asked if I would trust her to give me a haircut. When I agreed she started to lift my hair about, and then picked up a pair of scissors and began cutting it. She was obviously a lady of many talents, at least, I hoped so. Chunks of hair began dropping to the floor. 'Too late now.' I thought. could be I am going to lunch bald.' (*I began to feel quite lightheaded*) I was not allowed to see the result until she had finished drying and styling my hair and makeup.

Out came the makeup. A base was applied, and my face was contoured, cheeks highlighted, and a subtle blusher added. She moved on to my eyebrows, plucking them and pencilling in their shape. Green eye shadow and lash lengthening mascara followed. Double checking her work, Barbara asked me to cover my eyes while she walked me to a mirror. 'Tah Dah!' she said, 'you can look now.' I looked! Who was this woman in the mirror? I know I shouldn't say it, but I looked stunning. Barbara held up a hand mirror to show me the back of my hair. It looked beautiful. I did wonder whether I would be able to make it look the same myself though. I turned to Barbara and threw my arms around her, thanking her, I gave her a big hug. Barbara asked if she could go with me to my room and help me dress so she could see the overall result and take photos. Of course, I agreed.

We both gathered our things together and went to see Matron to thank her and her staff. Matron jokingly asked who I was, and I told her I was Madam Droopy Drawers, but she could call me Droops. After more thanks and hugs, we headed to my room. Time was now getting on;

lunch was in about an hour. I unlocked the door and in we went. Barbara moved to the wardrobe and after a couple of minutes she withdrew a coat hanger with a green dress, adding that it would be perfect. She insisted I put it on and pose or her so she could take a few photos. I gave her my mobile phone number and email address so she could send some of the photos over to me. Barbara said she would leave me to it and with promises to keep in touch, another hug and thank you, she left.

I still had fifteen minutes before I needed to go the canteen, I got my suitcase out and started chucking things in willy nilly. I left it on the bed and went to join the others in the canteen.

Chapter 28

Fond Fairwells

Johnny and Betty were waiting for me and did a double take when they saw me. 'Blimey,' Betty said, 'you certainly wash up well!' I twirled around saying, I have been Barbara-ed.' I went on to explain what she had done as we walked together to 'our' table. We sat down and picked up the lunch menus. After a few minutes Tim Bucktoo came to take our order. 'Good day,' he said in greeting, 'it ith nith to see you again. Do you with to order? The thoup of the day ith Thpithy Parthnip and we do not have Thtuffed muthroomth.

I couldn't look the others in the eye. 'Thank you Tim,' I said, 'I would like Sausage and Mash please.' Betty decided to have the same and Johnny asked for the pie. 'Right,' said Tim, thaths two Thauthage and math and one Pie. Would you like any drinkth?' Johnny said we only wanted tea or coffee so he would get it himself. Tim left to go to the kitchen and while Johnny went to get our beverages, Betty and I looked up at each other. 'I am going to miss you so much,' I told Betty, 'But I will be pleased to be home for a few days. My cat will have forgotten who I am, and I'm sure my friend will be pleased to have some respite too.'

Johnny returned to our table with our drinks and sat down. Movement at the bar caught my eye and I noticed Chris Cross III was behind the bar. 'I see Chris is still receiving punishment.' I commented. Johnny leaned in to speak to Betty and me, 'He's going to be there longer, he took his father's car without permission and got caught for drink driving and having no driving licence, spent the night in jail. His father, as you can imagine is not at all happy and has stopped his allowance. Luckily, in a week he is being sent to a training camp. His father is hoping it will sort him out once and for all.'

Tim arrived back with our meals and placed them in front of us. 'Thauthage and Math twithe and one Pie. Enjoy your mealths' and walked away.

While we ate, we chatted about the time I had been there and the things that had happened. We had many laughs at some of them.

Betty and I didn't want a sweet, but, of course, Johnny did. He ordered Treacle Suet Pudding and custard. (Or should that be Treacle Thuet Pudding and Cuthtard.) When we had all finished, we wandered slowly back to my room, I put my bag down and we then went into the little garden at the back. I was surprised to see Rupert, Ben. Goldie, Tim and Paul waiting in the garden. 'We've come to say goodbye.' Goldie said, adding, 'I might not be ere when yah come back, Ben and me are going to anover base, 'e has been prompted.' I gave her a huge hug and wished her well. Ben came and shook my hand, 'Nice knowing you,' he said. 'I am hoping I can persuade Goldie to marry me. I will send you an invite to the wedding if I am successful.' She would be a fool to turn you down I told him, adding that she would make a beautiful bride. They left arm in arm, with Goldie waving over her shoulder. I did hope all would go well, because she has so much to offer the right man. Tim and Paul then stepped forward and also shook hands (with me, not each other!) With a 'have and good holiday' from Tim and 'Ssssee you sssssoon hopefully' from Paul. I thanked them.

Betty came and gave me the biggest hug goodbye telling me she and Johnny were off to work on the next Test

Site in the morning, so wouldn't see me until my holiday was over. Johnny confirmed her words, also hugging me and they both left. (*I had never felt so hugged out in my entire life!*)

That just left Rupert and me. He asked if I was still happy for him to go with me the next day. Nodding I gave him and quick kiss on the cheek, telling him I was really looking forward to spending time with him. The car will be here at 8.30 in the morning, I went on, so I thought we could stop around noon for a bit of lunch. I walked him to the door, taking my hand he kissed it and walked away, turning to call out that he would be back at 8.30 sharp in the morning.

Chapter 29

The Journey Home

Having woken early, I made myself a mug of tea in my special 'forget-me-not' mug. And checked that I had packed everything that was mine. When I finished my tea, I rinsed the mug and carefully packed it between my clothes in the suitcase. It was now 8.10am so I had a quick wash and got dressed in jeans and a loose top. At 8.25 there was a knock at my door, and I opened it to find Rupert standing there, smiling at me. 'The car is here,' he said, and picked up my suitcase asking if I was ready. Nodding I closed the door behind me, locked it and put the key under a stone by the front door as instructed.

The driver of the car took my suitcase from Rupert and placed it in the boot of the car. He introduced himself as Robin Hoodwinkler, saluted Rupert, and told us he had the directions to my house so we could sit back and relax. I asked him if we could stop around noon for a bite to eat. Nodding in agreement, he opened the back passenger door, and I climbed in followed by Rupert. It was roomy inside, so we were able to stretch our legs. There was also a mini bar inside with bottled water, orange or pineapple juice, biscuits, and posh crisps. Having closed the door, Rob, as he had asked us to call him, put on his peaked cap, started the engine and we were off.

Rupert and I chatted away, asking each other questions about likes and dislikes, where we had travelled, family, and, before we knew it, Rob was turning into the car park of the very pretty whitewashed house with roses around the door. A sign welcomed us to Rose Cottage Cafe.

Rob parked up, opened the passenger door, and assisted me out. He had removed his hat and held it against his chest with one hand, saying he felt sure we would find this café acceptable. We smiled in agreement and walked towards the door. The roses smelt divine. Looking over my shoulder, I noticed Rob had not moved. 'Come on.' I called, 'you need to eat too.' Rupert beckoned him, 'We don't wish stand on ceremony so come and sit with us. So it was that all three of us entered Rose Cottage Café. It was a little dark after being outdoors, but a plump, smiling lady came towards us. 'Good afternoon,' she said, 'Table for three?' We nodded and she led us towards at table by a window overlooking the garden, asking us to be seated, pointed out the menu was on the table. She asked us if we would like a drink while deciding, we all decided to have a cup of tea in the meantime. I chose a cheese and onion toastie and asked the others to excuse me while I visited the restroom. (*'Ladies' to you and me!*) I took a few minutes to freshen up, put a brush through my shortened hair and went back to the table. Our tea had arrived and as I sat down, a young lad came towards us carrying a large tray with our food. He introduced himself as Peter Pecker, put the tray on a stand and placed our plates before us. We had all chosen the cheese and onion toasty which was served with a bit of salad, including watercress, that tasted delicious with it. While we ate Rupert told me Mine Host was Mrs Polly Pecker, Mother to Peter, who was on holiday from school and was intending to go to Cookery School and Restaurant Management. He was just filling in time helping Ma Pecker, his Mum.

Rob told us his Mum was an excellent cook, only thing was, she was given to occasionally 'helping herself' to the ingredients she wanted. She had been fined a couple of times but had avoided a prison sentence by pretending she had sudden blackouts and didn't know what she was doing. In fact, she had 'thrown a blackout' during her latest court appearance, suddenly stiffening, then collapsing onto the floor. Chaos had ensued, a medic was brought in, Dr Charlie Chargealot, who took her pulse, looked under her eyelids, slapped her cheek, and said he would administer a restorative. Laughing, he continued, that brought her round. He then declared she should be taken home immediately so her own doctor could examine her. He surreptitiously winked at my Mum. It turned out they grew up together and he was 'not all that! The Magistrate, Justice Nononsense declared her innocent and closed the case. There were several of Mum's friends in court to support her, they all cheered loudly, which caused Justice Nononsense to call for silence, upon which eight people playacted by tip toeing out of the court shushing each other loudly. By now Rupert and I were laughing, trying not to be too loud and disturb other people. Meanwhile, Rob continued, Mum was helped up by Dr Chargealot, and leaning on his arm, she gingerly walked out of court. Thanking him, she shook his hand and joined her friends. Going on, he added he had an agreement with the shopkeeper to keep an eye on her when she went into his store, and to let him know she had 'acquired' and he would cover the cost. He had also asked her friends to make sure she kept her hands in her pockets when out with them. However, it turned out that they took turns shoplifting for her.

Later she was placed in an Old People's Home - 'Sunny Pines.' Unfortunately, she had taken to pilfering bits of jewellery from the other …. Umm … inmates, going from room to room. To ensure she was not thrown out, he had purchased some fake jewellery which the staff placed in full sight in the rooms. So, she pilfered and the staff, reclaimed the 'jewels' while she was having her dinner and replaced them back in the rooms. She had passed a year ago, but her memory lives on. Rob told us he missed her, but sometimes it was a good miss.

Ma Pecker, as we now thought of her, came to the table, and asked if we would like more tea and perhaps a cake or two. We all agreed we would like more tea and, yes, cakes sounded good. We invited Ma to join us at the table and have tea with us. Looking around the room and seeing everyone seemed happed she agreed. She called Peter over and asked him to fetch tea and cakes.

While we were waiting we introduced ourselves to her and explained who we were and why we were travelling together. Rob briefly explained about his mother, which set us all off laughing again. Ma asked Rupert what he did or a living and when he told her he was an airman she patted his hand saying she lost her father during the war and it was her mother who started a cafe in a van to earn some money to keep them all. It became very popular, and after a couple of years she rented a café and served good homemade food at a reasonable price. She named the café 'Peckers Place.' Any food left over each night would be taken to a local hostel for servicemen who were going through hard times.

She explained that when she was old enough, she would help her mother in the café. Times began to change and the Café began to welcome a better clientele, which earned more money. Then her mother met someone who was to become her second husband. He had visited the café and they became friends. When he proposed, they were all amazed to learn he was quite wealthy. He owned Rose Cottage and after they married, the family moved in. He was older than mother and she was widowed again three years later. It was then she decided to turn Rose Cottage into a Café/Restaurant, and the rest is history. She left it to Ma as she had been helping her run it even though she was married herself with children. She ended by saying that there she was all those years later. She added that she would like Peter to marry and take over from her. She has a cosy little flat upstairs and was looking forward to just doing what she wanted when she wanted, but she realised it was a few years away yet. She had help from her niece Patsy Pattercake. Rob asked Ma if Patsy would be able to take over Rose Cottage for a day or so. Rupert and I looked at each other, both of us wondering where this was going. Ma thought for a while and replied she could certainly ask her, but why? Rob smiled and told her he would like to call in on his way back to the Base. It turned out his mother had taught him to cook and as he would be retiring in a month, he wondered whether he could perhaps offer his services as a cook/chef a few days a week, allowing Ma to take time off to meet up with friends or simply spend the day watching tv or reading. He would show Ma what he could cook and perhaps learn from her too. As you can imagine, Rupert and I were sitting without mouths wide open. (*I don't think my mouth has ever been wide open so many times as in this book.*)

Ma gave it some thought, then she looked towards us and asked our opinion of Rob. I admired her for asking our opinion in front of him. Rupert told her he was happy to couch for Rob. He was an honourable man, had worked for the RAF for many years and was trusted by the top brass. Having heard that, Ma agreed to Rob's suggestion. She stood up saying she must get back to work. Rupert asked for the bill, which was soon paid by him and with fond farewells, we went back to the car. On went Rob's hat, he opened the passenger door and both Rupert and I got in. 'On we go.' called Rob – and on we went!

Rupert and I quietly discussed what had just happened and, we concluded, it had nothing to do with us even though we were gobsmacked.

Our meal seemed to make us both sleepy and we gave in and slept, neither of us awakening until Rob called out 'Fanny, we are entering your road.' We both shot up and looked around. Yes, I thought, I am home. When Rob drew up and stopped outside my house, he got out, opened our door, and then went to the boot of the car to retrieve our luggage. He was in working mode, as he had his hat on.

Chapter 30

'Here you are at last!' called Ginny from the front door, 'I've shut Tigerfeet (my cat) in the kitchen, so she doesn't run out into the road.' I turned and waved to her, then, turning back to Rob, I invited him in for a coffee. 'I won't thank you,' he said, 'as I am calling into Rose Cottage on the way back. I wish you both a good holiday. Hope to see you both before I finally retire.' I couldn't stop myself; I hugged him and wished him all the best for the future. Rupert shook his hand, thanking him, and slipped him a few notes to pay for a meal on his way back.

We then turned to go up the front path and into the door which was being held open by Ginny. She smiled as we approached and led us into the kitchen. I could hear Tigerfeet scrabbling at the door and when she opened it he rushed out at seemingly 90 miles an hour to greet me. For a while I couldn't move because he was wrapping himself around my ankles. I bent down to pick him up for a cuddle. Meanwhile Ginny and Rupert were introducing themselves to each other. I put my cat down and despite him not agreeing to this plan. I held out my arms and Ginny walked into them. She gestured towards the table, suggesting we sit down. There were flowers in a vase in the centre of the table together with a plate of cakes. 'I didn't know if you would be hungry,' she said, 'but I do know you always have room for a cake. What would you like to drink?' Rupert and I asked for tea, and when made and passed to us, we sat around the table. Ginny was asking us lots of questions about what I had been doing which, unfortunately, I was unable to answer truthfully, but I did tell her about my horse -riding experience and the chattering on the bus. Rupert started to explain how we met, saying it was in the Naafi, when there was a knock at the door. Ginny went to answer it – it was Mrs Clara Carbunkle, who said, 'I saw the car arrive to drop Fanny and her friend off. I've got the room ready for her gentleman friend and thought I would just pop in to let her know.' 'Come in Clara,' I called. 'You are just in time for a cup of tea and cakes.' I smiled at Rupert, saying quietly, 'are you ready for this.'

In swept Clara, a picture in purple. She was an imposing figure, and I couldn't help thinking that if I looked like that at her age, I would be very happy, she had silver hair, with a purple rinse of course. Full makeup; purple eyeshadow and lipstick. Her dress was mid length with a pale lilac background with vivid purple flowers. She had a necklace around her neck with large mock pearl beads. The whole ensemble was only marred by the old-fashioned slippers on her feet. Noticing I was looking at them, she told me she went for comfort at home these days.

Chapter 31

Rupert meanwhile was standing, waiting to be introduced, but Clara gave me no time to do so as she swept forward and wrapped him in her arms. (*Even more bloody hugging.*) 'Well,' she said, 'Aren't you a fine figure of a man?' Rupert, looking rather startled, grinned at her and said he was very pleased to meet her. I asked Clara to sit down and, while Ginny was making her tea, Rupert answered her questions about himself. When she began to ask what meals he would like each day, he looked towards me questioningly. I explained to Clara that he would only need breakfast as the rest of the day we would be together and would get meals as we wanted them. 'Breakfast it is then.' Clara agreed and conversation went back to what I had been doing and then became more general. In a break in the conversation Clara asked 'Have you heard about Rev McPious? My sister, Petunia, told me. (Of course, I thought, Clara and Petunia do look very alike.) We all shook our heads and Clara continued to say that he and his wife had had a row to beat all rows and she packed her bags and left him. All the neighbours heard it. It seems Sarah had been carrying on with the said to be well endowed and very well-off Freddy Fortescue-Getsup. She and Freddy are now on their way to the South of France where he has a chateau. 'Goodness me!' Ginny exclaimed, 'when did Aunt Petunia come to see you?' 'She didn't' Clara replied, 'she phoned me. She said it served McPious right. Word is going round that he imbibes several bottles of wine a week, some of which are Communion wine. Sarah helps him to bed, then he passes out and she sneaks off to meet Freddy. They have also been seen together in a Pub in Upper

Theadbare. However, according to her neighbours, that night McPious was awake when she crept back in after an assignation and all hell broke loose. He called her several nasty names, so she punched him in the eye and he fell back on the bed. Sarah pulled a suitcase off the top of her wardrobe and started throwing things in it. She took most of her jewellery except for her wedding and engagement rings, her bank cards, passport, etc. Followed by summer clothes, makeup, not forgetting the teddy bear given to her when she was born. She phoned Freddy to come and collect her and twenty minutes later she was gone. McPious had sat and watched all this going on, seeming unable to move.

'Well,' I said, 'seems there was a lot of excitement while I was away. What happened to the Vicar?' Clara said that he had been reprimanded and was under close scrutiny by church officials, which made us all chuckle. 'No more communion wine for him then.' said Rupert.

Ginny started to clear the table, putting our plates and mugs into the dishwasher. I suggested Clara take Rupert to see his room, unpack and whatever and then come back here. After they had left, Ginny said, 'Well, well, well, he seems like a nice fella. How long is he staying?' 'Two weeks,' I said, 'then we will take it from there. 'O.k.,' Ginny said, 'I'll be off now. I'm going away for a few days tomorrow, so I'll see you when I return. I asked her where she was going and she said she and a friend were off to Centre Parks, we love it there. I thanked her profusely and wished her a brilliant holiday. Pulled an envelope from my purse and gave it to her saying it was a thank you from me. Ginny didn't want to accept it, but I insisted she did so, and then she left.

Chapter 30

Now I had a few minutes to myself I sat at the table to think things over. I realised how much I had missed my home. It was like I had been on holiday, and although I had enjoyed myself, I didn't want to go away again for a while. Getting up, I picked up my suitcase and headed upstairs. I began to unpack, putting things away or into the washing basket. I then went into the bathroom to have a quick shower and a change of clothes. I reckoned I had about an hour before Rupert returned. I began to feel excited at the thought of the next couple of weeks.

I had just returned downstairs when the front door opened, and Rupert entered. It seemed so right to have him walk through my door. We smiled each other and I invited him to come and sit with me in the lounge. It was 7.00pm by now and the weather was balmy. I asked how he had got on with Clara, his reply made me laugh. 'Well,' he said, 'I was instructed to leave my luggage in the hall and to go through to the kitchen with her. She pointed out where everything was so I could make a drink whenever I want. She then led me into the dining room and showed me a table under the window where my breakfast would be served.' 'Bless her,' I said. He carried on, 'There is a bowl of fruit on the sideboard, and I am to help myself whenever I want some. After I thanked her, she took me upstairs to a very feminine room with an ensuite. She then showed me where the spare towels are, then, after I paid her for a week's stay, which she said was unnecessary, but thanked me for, she left. I have a double bed that feels very comfortable. I did wonder whether she had given me her bedroom, but later I caught sight of another bedroom through its open door, and it looked bigger than mine.

I took a quick shower after unpacking, I found she had left a front door key on my bedside table so I could let myself in without disturbing her.

Rupert had dressed casually as he was unsure what we would be doing. I suggested we took a walk and perhaps call in at a pub for a bite to eat. I quickly fed Tigerfeet, who had decided Rupert had just the right sort of lap to curl up on, which I took as a good sign. I went to get a cardigan and put on a pair of comfortable walking shoes. Leaving the house, we took the walk towards Lower Threadbare. On the way, I told Rupert about Aunty Peculiar, as she was known, and her vendetta against the Vicar. The same one Clara had spoken about. We walked past the Church, and I pointed out Aunt Peculiar's back garden. The washing line was empty unfortunately. We continued along Blanketstitch Lane and took Sewing Street towards Upper Threadbare.

By now we were holding hands and only spoke when we saw something of interest, feeling so comfortable with the silences. When we reached Needle Road, which is the main street, we stopped to look at several paintings in the window of Arty Crafty Gallery. Rupert was very drawn to a portrait of the local Smithy at work in his Blacksmith Shop. 'I can almost feel the heat.' He said, 'Is there a Smithy here?'

I led him down a back street and showed him the building belonging to Bright Spark Blacksmith. Proprietor: Silas Shoesmith.

'I would like to come and watch him work one day if possible. I see he is open between 8.00am and 8.00pm Monday to Friday and 8.00am to 12 noon Saturday.' Closed Sundays. 'I'm sure we can,' I replied. 'I love the noise and the smell when the Smithy is working. As I said that Silas Shoesmith came walking towards his Smithy. 'Good evening,' he said, 'can I be of help to you?' Rupert held out his hand and introduced himself – Rupert, I am here on holiday and would love to watch you work.' 'You can watch now if you wish, there is a horse that has thrown a shoe and it is on its way here. In fact, would you like to man the bellows for me so we can be one step ahead and have a good fire going before the horse arrives.' Ruperts face lit up, he looked towards me, and I told him to go ahead, I would enjoy watching.

The fire was alight, and the heat was amazing. Rupert took off his jumper and worked the bellows like a 'goodun'. Silas donned his leather apron and checked his anvil was clean. When the fire reached the correct heat Silas began to work on the horseshoe. He had already gathered the nails needed.

The bell rang outside, and Silas called 'Come on in, Dave, I am all ready for you.' Dave led in one of the most beautiful horses I have ever seen. I asked if I could stroke it and Dave nodded his head in agreement. He told me her name was Lady Grace of Lowlands. She is a prize-winning Arabian mare and is in foal at present. To say she was beautiful, was an understatement. She had a gentle nature and the longest tail on a horse I had ever seen. Silas asked for her to be brought to him and he moved around to her back, picked up the foot with the loose shoe and removing the nail, took the shoe off.

'Keep pumping Rup,' he called, 'I just need to shape the shoe to fit the horse.' Moving back to the anvil, he picked up his smith hammer and after placing the shoe into the coals until it became red hot, and the clanging sound began. When he was happy with the shape he doused it in a bucket of water, making a hissing sound. He then once again lifted the Mare's hoof and checked the shoe was a good fit, then applied it using nails he had been holding in his mouth.

The old horseshoe was laying on the ground and Silas picked it up and handed it to Rupert, who was really chuffed. We turned and watched Lady Grace being led out the door.

We both thanked Silas so much, Rupert saying it was one of the best experiences of his life and he would never forget it.

Chapter 32

Walking back to Needle Road, with Rupert clutching his horseshoe, I suggested we pop into the Pub at the end of the road, The Needle & Thread for a beer and a bite to eat, and then head back home. A menu was posted by the front door, and we stood for a while studying this and having decided, went inside. It was very busy, so we headed for the bar to get a drink and soup each and, also ask for a table. A table was eventually found for us. We didn't know it was Karaoke night until someone started to sing 'Why, why, why, Deliah.' We sat awaiting our soup with a roll.

Delilah came to a finish and the next singer stepped onto the stage. She sang an Adele song.

Our soup arrived to the accompaniment of 'Do you think I'm Sexy?' He was rather overweight and got boo'ed off the stage before the end of the song. The next song was 'Can't Live, if living is without you.' sung by another man, who did have a good voice.

We had just finished our soup when another rendition of 'Why, why, why Delilah began. I looked at Rupert and nodded my head towards the door, smiling, he agreed, and we both stood up and left. It was now rather dark, and we hurried back home. Rupert didn't come in but gave me a quick kiss goodnight and headed across to Clara's. I watched until he unlocked her door and, after waving to me, went in.

The following morning, after a good night's sleep, I was up and about early. While waiting for Rupert t arrive, I had a look online to see if I could find somewhere interesting to visit that were not too far away. The first place I found was a Country Park with animals, a train that wove in and out the grounds and we could also visit the house, Mockingham Manor.

I also found an airfield that provided Hot Air Balloon Rides. I didn't know whether Rupert has been up in a balloon, but I certainly hadn't and would really like to.

I heard the front door open, and Rupert entered calling or a cheerful good morning. I let him know I was in the kitchen trying to find places to visit. Giving me a quick peck on the cheek he sat down. I noticed we were both wearing jeans and sweatshirts so whatever we did today, we were suitable dressed. I showed him the two things I had chosen so far, asking if either of them appealed to him. 'Both do,' he said, 'I have never been up in a hot air balloon, as strange as that may sound. How about you?' 'No, I haven't either, but the thought of just quietly drifting high up in the air and looking down on the houses and fields sounds really exciting.'

Knowing these rides were usually booked well in advance I thought we could perhaps be lucky enough to book a cancellation. Rupert agreed, and picking up my mobile I phoned the number and put speaker phone on. The conversation went as follows: -

Them: Good morning, Higher Up Hot Air Balloons, how can I help you?

Me: Good morning, I am ringing to enquire if you have free rides this week.

Them: I regret, we do not give rides for free.

Me: No, I meant have you any balloon rides for two people this week.

Them: I will check for you.

Me: Thank you.

Them: I have checked, we have one couple booked this week.

Me: Umm, you are not understanding. I would like to book a hot air balloon ride for me and a friend this week if you have space for us.

Them: Do you weigh very heavy that you ask if there is space for you, and your friend also?

Me: (By now we were finding it difficult not to laugh and Rupert's face was a picture.) No, neither of us is overweight. I meant have you any vacant places this week.

Them: Vacant places, what are these? I am a bit on the slow side, but I wouldn't call myself vacant.

Me: I think I need to speak to the Manager please.

Them: No, no. no. no! Sorry, please do not speak to the Manager to report me. I am already in trouble for answering the phone yesterday. I will be sacked if I am found to have done it again.

Me: (breathing deeply) Is the Manager there? If so, can you put the phone down and I will dial the number again. Please do not answer it yourself.

Them: Yes ok. I do that. The phone clicked down.

I took a couple of minutes to get my breath, then redialled. I rang for quite a while before it was answered.

Them: Good Morning, Higher Up Hot Air Balloons.

Yes, you got it, it was answered in the same foreign accent. I cancelled the call.

'Seems we will not be hot air ballooning,' I said to Rupert, laughing. And off to Mockingham Manor we went.

The next few days passed very quickly. We learned a lot about each other and found we had the same interests too. We spent a great deal of time walking around local beauty spots, mostly eating out.

Chapter 33

However, on the Monday of the second week Rupert arrived looking very excited. 'Fanny,' he called, 'I have something important to discuss with you. 'Oh what?' I asked. He took out his mobile phone saying he had received a message this morning and he handed it to me to read.

Senior Rupert Allman

'Good Morning,

This message is important and needs to be answered soonest.

The position of Wing Commander at Airbase Benevolent has become vacant and we would like to discuss this position with you a.s.a.p. Wing Commander Kamikarzi is being put in charge of our Top-Secret Development Department, continuing the work he has already carried out. Wing Commander Bouncers will become his second in command. You have been recommended for this position and we need to fill it within two weeks.

Please be available tomorrow at 10.00am, when a car will be sent to collect you.

Air Vice Marshall Topman-Gallant'

As I read this, my heart dropped. It seemed our holiday together was over. 'How wonderful for you,' I said, 'have you made any sort of decision?' Rupert replied that he wanted to talk it over with me first, but even if he were to turn down this opportunity, he was duty bound to attend the meeting. He continued that there was no way he would accept if I was unhappy. 'But .....,' I started. Rupert put a finger over my mouth, asking me to listen.

'We have spent a week together now and I am even more sure we belong together.' He dropped to one knee asking, 'Fanny Fernickety, would you do me the honour of accepting my hand in marriage?' for a few seconds I just stood there and then answered 'Yes, oh, yes!' Rising to his feet, Rupert took me into his arms and kissed me. My legs turned to jelly, as Rupert picked me up and swung me round and round. Breathless and giggling, I asked him to stop because I was beginning to feel a bit sick. When he heard that, he stopped immediately and took a step back. 'You've done that to me once already and I didn't enjoy it.' he said, smiling.

We both sat down, and Rupert asked if I would be happy to move to nearer the Base. I didn't have to think about it, so I told him I would have no problem with that. I really didn't have anything here to hold me back. Tigerlegs would soon get used to it, and I could always come back to visit with my friends, or they could come to me. I began to feel very excited. Not only was I going to marry, but I was going to live in an area I had fallen in love with.

Rupert answered his message in the affirmative, and we then tried to sort out what should be done first. Obviously the first person to speak to would be Clara to let her know her room was no longer needed. Rupert would pay her extra as he felt it was only fair.

I went to get a notepad and pen, so I could write everything down.

1. Put my house on the market
2. Get packing boxes
3. Contact a Removals Company with storage
4. Go through my clothes, send what I don't want to charity

5. Go through everything in the house and decide what to keep and what to send to charity.
6. Sort out that cupboard under the stairs.
7. Contact services, electricity gas etc.
8. Cancel telephone and Internet

We decided to get married in a registry office near the Base and Rupert would make the arrangements. I was to make a list of those I would like to invite. We could hold the reception in the Naafi.

Rupert apologised for having to leave at such short notice, and promised he would keep me up to date with everything. He would return as soon as he could, depending on what the promotion entailed. If necessary, if he was unable to come to me, I could go to him. He added that there was accommodation available on the Base, but he, personally would rather live nearby, like most places where people work and live in close proximity rumours were rife, and the gossip mill can cause a lot of trouble. That will be my priority during my off time, to find us somewhere to live, even if we rent for a while and look around together. He added that he wanted to start our lives together on the right foot.

And so, the next morning, Clara and I stood on my doorstep to wave goodbye to Rupert. I knew I was really going to miss him, but hopefully it would not be for too long.

I phoned the Estate Agents, Lord, Lord and Deville, their motto being 'Sell or Buy, Give Us a Try,' and who handled my purchase of this house very professionally. Their Representative was to call the next morning, so that was one thing off my list.

Next was packing boxes. I looked on my local Market Place and found several people had boxes on offer. I contacted a woman who lived near to me and bought four tea chests and several cardboard boxes. They were not expensive as she had used them herself. She promised her husband would drop them off for me the next day in his van, and he would collect the money. Number two sorted.

I bypassed number three for the time being until I had a definite date.

Chapter 34

Sorting out clothes follows. I decided to message Ginny and ask her to come over and help me decided what to keep and what not. I soon had an answer from her, she was in the local Supermarket 'Costa Lotta' and would call in on her way home – with cake! Smiling, I went upstairs and started to take things out of my wardrobe and laid them on my bed. There were several outfits I knew I wanted to keep, but I would leave the rest until Ginny arrived. I went downstairs to put the kettle on ready for a coffee for us both.

Within a few minutes Ginny arrived sans cake. We sat at the kitchen table with our drinks enjoying double chocolate cake. I told her all about my time with Rupert and, of course, our engagement. She told me she thought something like that would happen and she was thrilled for me. Having eaten
our cake and finished our drink we headed off upstairs. I indicated the outfits I had decided to keep, then the ones I was not sure of. In the corner were the ones I had already decided should go. Ginny asked if she could try on the 'go-ers' when we had finished, I nodded my head, and we started sorting the 'not sures.'

Two hours later we sat on the bed surrounded by 'keepers,' looking at the pile of 'go-ers.' I had been down to get us a glass of wine each and as we sat sipping, I told Ginny that I would hang my 'keeper' back up and then she could attack the 'go-ers.' It is amazing how quickly a person could drink a glass of wine when they wanted. Ginny looked at me, hiccupped, and asked if she could make a start. Permission given; she picked up a red dress I know she has envied since I bought it. She tried it on, and it really did look better on her. Ginny now had her own 'keepers' and 'go-ers.' At the end, the piles for about fifty-fifty. We put the 'go-ers' in a black bag for charity, and I went to the cupboard under the stairs and pulled out suitcase I had used when I first went to the Base, and we packed Ginny's Keepers' inside. Dragging the bag of 'go-ers' downstairs ready to be taken to the Charity Shop around the corner in Leftover Lane. Of course, the shop was called Leftover Charity Goods.

Ginny left carrying her bounty with her, promising to come back in a couple of days to help me start packing. As she left, a van arrived, and the driver got out, opened the back doors, and started to bring me the tea chests and cardboard boxes I had asked for. I quickly went into the kitchen to get the money for him. He also had a roll of tape to make the boxes up with, which I thought was very thoughtful. He thanked me and wished me good luck. As he drove away, I went online and ordered a large roll of bubble wrap for next day delivery.

I made up one of the smaller boxes and went into the front room to start culling the ornaments. Looking around the room, I realised this was going to be more difficult than I thought, so I decided to have a couple of pieces of toast and marmite and a cup of tea. I had just sat down when my mobile rang. It was Rupert to let me know he had arrived, and he was already missing me. He has his interview tomorrow morning, and in the meantime, he would be checking the local papers for flats to rent. I told him about Ginny's visit, the Estate Agents visit the next day and the tea chests and boxes. We chatted or a while, and when my front doorbell rang, we decided to say goodbye, sending our love to each other and I walked up the hall to see who was there.

To my surprise, it was Clara.' Hello again,' I said, 'do come in.' Clara apologised for troubling me, but she had heard I was putting my house on the market, and she had a dear friend who wanted to buy a property in this area. I told her the Estate Agent man would coming the next day to put a price on the property and as soon as I knew what it was, I would let her know. I realised the front room would have to wait until tomorrow.

I fell into bed that night, I had so much on my mind I thought I wouldn't sleep, but as soon as my head hit the pillow, I was off into the land of nod.

The Estate Agent's agent, Mickail DeMorgan, arrived promptly at 10.30am. I invited him in and he started in the kitchen, eyes everywhere, I don't think he missed a thing. Then into the front room. He was very quietly talking into a small recording thing, about the size of a mobile phone, so I couldn't hear what he was saying. He looked around the hall and then headed upstairs. He went first into my bedroom; luckily, I had made the bed as soon as I got up, more talking into microphone, good look in the bathroom, and the second bedroom. Going back downstairs, he told me he would go back to the office and would ring me with a price in the afternoon. (*I need to add that I didn't totally understand what he said, because he had a strong foreign accent. However, I did glean that he was going to phone me later.*) He left calling 'Goodbye Madam,' leaving me in the hall with my mouth wide open.

Chapter 35

Once more I entered the lounge to sort out ornaments, etc. As I said, it was very hard as a lot of the things belonged to my Mum and Dad. However, I decided to choose just three things they had left me. I had a couple of antiques, which I would send to be auctioned at Sellers Antiques a few miles away. If they made good money, it would pay for the removal and storage of the rest of my goods. I started to put all my things into the box so I could carry it out to the kitchen and sort them in there. I also collected ornaments from all over the house, many of which were rather dusty.

Two hours later I have six things on the table which I am vacillating over which to keep. I couldn't believe it took that long to sort them out, and I kept seeing other things I really loved. I added another two, telling myself I needed them. I quickly put all the others back into the cardboard box and stuck the lid down so I would not be tempted to get out more. The items I saved are:

- An angel my dad bought my Mum when I was born.
- A brass horse and cart I bought Dad because he always wanted a pony and trap.
- A little glass bell I was allowed to ring so Mum would come and see me when I felt unwell and was in bed.
- A wooden teddy bear.
- A buddha with a large tummy that I would rub in the belief I would receive riches.
- A sophisticated lady statue I bought from a second-hand shop when I was into Flappers

- My netball trophy from school because it was the only thing I had ever won in the whole of my schooldays.
- My Dad's retirement watch.

I decided I would keep all eight items, so I put them on a shelf in the front room while I waited for the bubble wrap to arrive.

My mobile phone rang, it was Mickail from the Estate Agents. When he told me the selling price of my house, I was very pleased. It was worth quite a lot more than I thought. I gave him instructions to put it on the market. I immediately phoned Clara and told her, who said she would pass it on to her friend. We chatted for a few minutes about what I had already done to prepare to leave, and about her friend who was hoping to come down here to live. Telling me she would let me know whether her friend was interested, we said goodbye.

.

Chapter 36

Next on my list was the cupboard under the stairs. Opening it I looked in. 'Oh dear,' I thought, 'this is going to take ages too. Leaning in I took out the personal file which I then put in the front room to be packed. Looking at the clock, I saw it was now five o'clock in the evening and I needed to eat. I decided to walk to Codpiece Fish & Chips shop, which was about 2 miles away. On the way I met up with another friend, Sarah, and I stopped to chat with her for a while. She had recently married one of our school friends, Henry (Hopeless) Harper. I got the feeing she was rather regretting it, as she said his name really suited him. 'What, Henry?' I asked. 'No,' she replied, his nickname Hopeless, because according to her, he was even more hopeless than she knew before she married him. He was a walking disaster she told me; he had broken a window in the kitchen by accidently pushing a ladder into it. He was supposed to be putting it against the wall to clean the upstairs windows but tripped over a brick and through the window it went. He then tripped over and broke his ankle and was hopping around arms flailing knocking stuff on the floor. She was out for a walk she said because she was close to throttling him. I began to feel sorry for Henry. I remembered him from school, and he was one of the kindest boys there was. Yes, he was accident prone, but he was still very popular among the other boys. As we walked on Sarah confided in me that she thought she was pregnant, and it seemed to make her very short tempered. Poor Henry!

At the next corner we parted company, and I walked on towards the Fish Shop. I had heard it had changed hands a couple of weeks ago and I was interested to see if it was good as it used to be. When I reached the shop,

I saw people were queueing outside it. I joined the queue and the conversation of two women in front of me caught my attention.

Woman 1: You missed an argument at choir last night.

Woman 2: Really, what happened?

Woman 1. Cecily thought she was going to be the lead singer of the opening song, but Humphry gave it to the newcomer, Chloe Jones. You haven't met her, but she is young and very pretty and also has a better voice than Cecily.

Woman 2. So, what happened after that?

Woman 1. Cecily demanded to know how someone who had just joined the choir should be offered such an opportunity. After all, she only joined this evening and as far as we know, she can't sing for toffee. Humphry held up his hand and asked her to please be quiet and pointed out that Chloe recently won a singing competition and has a lot of experience in performing in front of an audience.

Woman 2. Bet that went down a storm.

Woman 1. Storm, more of a cyclone! Cecily grabbed the song sheets out of Humphry's hand and threw them up in the air. That caused the other choir members to erupt. Cecily was called several fruity names. Agatha and her daughter demanded Cecily leave, which cause Cecily to pick up a couple of hymn books and throw them at Cecily. Poor Chloe just stood there watching the chaos going on around her.

(We moved a bit closer to the door)

Woman 2. What are your feelings about it?

Woman 1. To be honest I was rather gleeful. Cecily Snobhead ....

Woman 2 interrupted, laughingly saying Snobhead? Don't you mean Snowhead?

Woman 1, Whatever, she thinks she's better than the rest of us, having been married to a Colonel. Anyway, Snobhead told me the other day I should try to lose weight cos I took up two spaces on the bench.

Woman 2. Cheeky Cow, she's so skinny she would fall through a drain in the gutter if she wasn't careful.

(They were now both inside the shop)

Woman 1. Well, Humphry started shouting for quiet, Cecily picked up another hymn book and threw it at him. That's when the riot started. There were hymn books being thrown by several people. Old John was a very good shot, having bowled for the County Cricket Club and he caught Cecily a goodun on the back of the head. She fell into Humphry, who staggered back and knocked a box of candles on the floor. Meanwhile Cecily was trying to keep on her feet but, unfortunately, the candles started to roll towards the guttering in the floor by the pews and she stepped on one and went headlong into the large flower arrangement just inside the door.

(I was now inside the door)

Woman 2. I wish I had seen all this. What happened then?

Woman 1. Someone called the Police and Cecily and Humphry were taken to the Police Station to be interviewed. I have not heard the outcome, but Cecily's last words were you can shove your choir where the sun don't shine, I am never coming here again. This caused cheers from the rest of the choir, many of whom met up at the Right Royal Ruckas and old John didn't have to buy a drink all night. My hubby was there, and he said it was one of the best evenings he had ever had. The choir members were singing sea shanties, some of which had the words changed to profane ones.

Woman 2. (Who was now at the counter asked for Cod and Chips twice.) She then turned to Woman 1 and asked if the choir was still going to continue.

Woman 1. Don't know to be honest, I'm, sure we'll hear soon enough.   (She turned to order two battered sausages, a fish cake and one portion of chips please.)

The two of them left the shop together still discussing the choir.

I asked for Huss and Chips, paid, and walked home at a much faster pace, laughing at what I had just heard.

When I reached home, I shared my fish with Tigerfeet and sat down eating hungrily.

Chapter 37

Rupert phoned me at eight and we chatted about our days. His interview went very well, and he had permission to come down and stay overnight so he could discuss the outcome with me. 'I will be with you about eleven tomorrow if that is ok' he said, 'I will return back here the following afternoon.'

He would be bringing a couple of rental flat details for me to see. He added that we should think about opening a joint bank account that we could pay into to cover rent, etc. but added we could talk about it tomorrow.

He had spoken to the Chaplain of the Base, and he would be pleased to marry us, rather than in a Registry Office. Another thing to discuss the next day.

As you can imagine, I was delighted to know he would be coming the next day. I decided he could stay with me (in the spare room, or his clothes could!)

I decided to try to tackle the cupboard under the stairs. I had some black bags and decided I would put everything any good into them to be taken to the charity shop. In the first bag I put the old handbags, all the craft stuff, bri- a-brac and the Christmas decorations. I decided to double up the black bags so I could put the golf club and the guitar in it without the bag tearing. I put both bags back in the cupboard for now. This done I headed upstairs to get ready for bed.

I awoke early the next morning, smiling as I remembered Rupert would be coming today. Before eight o'clock I had changed the bedding, put a wash on, showered and dressed. While making a mug of tea and some toast, I looked for a business card given to me by a young lad up the road. He had a hand cart and offered his services to take heavy packages to the Post Office, or sacks of potatoes to families in the area, etc, and I was hoping he would be willing to take my two bags to the Charity Shop. Finding the card, I gave the number a ring. His Mum answered saying that he was still in bed, but she would get him up and he would be with me within the hour. I looked again at his card to remind myself of his name. I read, Davy Jones – a boy with a cart. Anything that fits in the cart can be transported to anywhere in the Village. £10.00 within a two-mile radius.

True to her word, Davy was knocking my door within half an hour. I invited him in to show what I had and told him where it was to go. We agreed a price of £12.00 as the Charity Shop was a bit further away. I helped him by carrying one bag to the cart while he took the other. When he saw the guitar Davy asked if he could keep it for himself. I happily agreed and he told me I only need pay him £10 now.

'Bless him,' I thought handing over a £10 note. It was then I remembered the 'goers' upstairs in a bag. I asked if he had room for another bag in his cart, to go to the same place. He agreed he would only ask for a further five pounds. Upstairs I went to get the bag of goers and another three pounds in payment. Davy loaded the extra bag onto his cart, accepted the three pounds and headed off, whistling very loudly. By now the washing was done and I put it into a laundry basket to enable me to carry it outside. It was rather dull, but I thought I'd take a chance as it was quite windy, which, with a bit of luck, will dry the washing before it does rain. (*Luckily it did*)

Just enough time to put on some makeup and I'm ready.

It's now eleven o'clock and I'm in my front room watching for Rupert's arrival. And there is the car. I ran to the door, opened it, and called Rupert's name. He was just lifting his case from the boot of the car. He turned and smiled at me. Thanking his driver, who was to collect him tomorrow, he wasted no more time coming to meet me. Putting down his luggage, he took me into a big bear hug, telling me how much he had missed me. Saying I felt the same, I led him into the house. He left his luggage in the hall and followed me into the kitchen. I invited him to sit down while I made us a drink. These made, I sat at the table with him. He started to explain all that had happened and how much he would love to take up the offer of promotion. He had given it a great deal of thought and decided that in the end, although he would be sorry to give up his involvement in the Stealth Drone, he knew that being with me was what he really wanted.

He told me more about his family. His parents had died in a car crash when he was very young. An Aunt had taken him in and raised him. She too was no longer with us, and he then found another family in the Airforce, who look after each other despite everything. Marrying me would make his life even better, as when he was with me, he felt he was home. I understood completely what he meant, as I no longer had parents or grandparents and life is very lonely without them.

Rupert got up and went to his luggage, bring a file back with him., telling me if we get all the decisions made, we can spend more time just being together.

He opened the file and the first thing he showed me was the details of the two flats he had found. The first was a ground floor one. It had two bedrooms, a nice bathroom, a fair-sized kitchen and a lounge with a door into the small garden at the back. It was in a quiet road, and he chose it as it would be ideal for Tigerfeet. There were shops nearby and a park. The rent was quite high, but we hopefully wouldn't be in it for too long. We can rent it for three months and renew if we haven't found somewhere to buy.

He then showed me the second flat, it was in a more built-up area, but was larger inside, as was the garden. Again, it was ground floor flat. Nearby was a Garden Centre, a Cinema, and a Shopping Centre. The rent was a little cheaper than the first flat. Rupert felt we should consider it though as I would be on my own a lot of the time during his first months of training. However, he knew I found it easy to make friends and there were also the people at the Base I knew. We could rent it for three months too.

Then he pulled out another paper. This was details of a house we could buy. I began to feel very excited at the thought. Rupert spread out the details in front of me. It was five miles from the Base set in its own grounds, albeit small. It had three bedrooms and bathroom upstairs and a toilet, a lounge and extended kitchen downstairs. There was a sunroom with access from the kitchen and the lounge. When I saw the price, I glanced at Rupert in askance. It was not a cheap property. Rupert explained that he had an inheritance from his parents that had been building interest for many years. He had never touched it as he knew that one day, he would need it. He had had everything he needed by being in the Airforce, and the time was now. He had taken the bull by the horns and made an appointment for both of us to view it tomorrow late afternoon. It will mean you travelling back with me tomorrow. 'Is there anyone who can come in if you have any views on your house booked?' he asked. When I told him a friend of Clara was looking for a property down here, he suggested I accept a lower offer from her.

'Let me talk to Clara,' I said, 'perhaps she has an answer from her friend by now. Why not come with me to see her because she will be disappointed if not.' I added.

As I thought, Clara was delighted to see Rupert again. We were invited in for a cup of tea and a piece of cake, and while she was making our drinks, I explained about my visit to see a house near the Base the next day. Clara said she was going to pop over and see me as she had heard from her friend who was hoping to come tomorrow to stay with Clara so she could look over my house and see the surrounding area. We agreed it would work out brilliantly, especially as Clara would love having her friend living near her. So, we hoped she would like the house and area. I told Clara I would post a front door key through her letterbox before leaving the next day.

After we had returned home, we talked about the best way to go about our finances. I explained that I had been made redundant from an accountancy position as the company was going into liquidation. That is why I answered the advert, because there are no jobs around here and a bit of cash would be helpful. It would be my intention to find work up there. Rupert insisted there was no hurry, he could well afford to keep us both. He suggested me getting a part time job if I wanted too, although it would be good to have me able to travel with him from time to time. He would have to go to conferences and such, although I wouldn't have to go every time. I thought it was a decision we could come to when we knew where we were and where we were living.

That being the case, he thought it would be better for the moment for us to keep our own bank accounts. After we are married, we would definitely need one from which to pay the bills.

Chapter 38

Time was now getting on and we decided, to head off to bed and decide together in the morning, what furniture we wanted to keep, if any, and what we didn't.

We didn't rush into things in the morning; We had a leisurely fried breakfast, and it was getting on for eleven o'clock before we were washed and dressed. I grabbed my notebook and pencil, and we went from room to room discussing what to keep and what should go. To be honest, there was not a lot we wanted to keep, especially as we would get an allowance from the Airforce to cover moving expenses. With that in mind the only piece of furniture I wanted to keep was a dressing table in the spare bedroom that had belonged to my Mum.

Rupert decided we should make up the boxes in readiness for packing. We were halfway through sorting the spare room when the bubble wrap arrived. This enabled me to protect my eight items I was going to keep safe from breakages. I packed these in one of the tea chests. To this I added some decent bedding and towels. I phoned a local charity shop that collected second hand furniture to ask them to see if there was anything they wanted before I took them to the dump. I would rather they went to somewhere they are really needed. They would be coming with their van at one thirty in the afternoon. I know it was running it rather tight, but the way things were moving forward, the sooner it was done the better.

Grabbing another box, I started to pack my crockery, saucepans, cutlery, etc. In another I put tea towels, small electrical goods, cooking items and anything else that was left.

Two hours later the furniture was loaded on their van together with the boxes from the kitchen and off they went. Rupert and I stood in the empty lounge in silence. I started to laugh and asked him not to jilt me at the altar as I had nothing left, even the beds were gone. Rupert phoned Clara and asked if I could stay with her until we married, and if so, could he bring my clothes, etc over, as all the furniture was gone. Bless her, she readily agreed and so we headed over to her house clutching all my worldly goods between us. Rupert went back to collect the tea chest and carried it upstairs. Clara told us not to worry, she would unpack everything I would need so when I came back in a couple of days, everything would be in place. Thanking her I handed her the spare front door key and asked her to please feed Tigerfeet and sit with him for a while, which she readily agreed to do, and Rupert and I headed back to the empty house.

We didn't have long to wait, the car arrived about fifteen minutes later. I had packed a few things for my overnight stay at the Base. Rupert had booked me into the same room I was in before.

We sat together in the back of the car holding hands, and it wasn't long before we both fell asleep. Our driver, Zac, woke us, saying we were about half an hour away from the Base, which was a bit of a shock – we must have been tired.

The car pulled up by my room and we both got out. Rupert carried our bags to the door and went back to thank and tip Zac. I found the key in its usual place under a stone, unlocked the door and went in followed by Rupert carrying our bags. I went to make us a cup of tea, luckily there two mugs and plenty of teabags, milk, and sugar sachets. 'Will you be staying here?' I asked, turning to look at him. 'That I will, if agreeable to you, seems silly not to.' We unpacked our things and Rupert suggested we went over to the Naafi for a meal. I agreed and, after I had given my hair a brush and put on a bit of lipstick, we strolled over together.

When we entered the building, we immediately went to what we felt was our table. 'Feels like I never left,' I said, 'Is the menu still the same?' Rupert nodded and as we were both hungry, picked up the menu to make a choice. 'I'm going to skip a starter and have the pie tonight., how about you?' 'I think I'll join you,' he said, 'what do you fancy to follow?' I decided to see how I felt after the pie, so when Tim Bucktoo came to our table with his pad to take our order. Good evening, Thir and Madam, may I take your order. Good Evening, Tim, no need to stand on ceremony, I am still the same Fanny, so please do not call me Madam. We would both like the pie please, and I'll have a glass of water, not sure about you,' I added, turning to Rupert. 'Make mine water too,' he said, 'need to keep a clear head for our house hunt tomorrow.'

'Oh, congratulathons to you both,' he said,' I with you many yearth of happineth.' And so saying, he left place our orders in the kitchen. Rupert grinned at me, saying I had better get used to being congratulated. Everyone was really pleased for us. This was proved to be true, as Ben and several others came to wish us well for the future. We accepted their good wishes and when Tim came to the table with our meals, they left, still loudly calling out their congratulations.

We settled down to enjoy our dinner, only talking occasionally, which showed how well we got on, not needing to fill any gaps with words. Feeling replete, neither of us had room for anything more, so indicating to Tim to bring the bill, he paid it, thanked him, gave him a tip.

Together we walked to our room, watched a bit of television, and decided to take an early night.

Chapter 39

We awoke early and took turns taking a shower. I put on a calf length dress that fit me very well, and a cardigan that picked up one colour from the dress. Rupert was smartly dressed too. Rupert told me we were going to a jeweller to pick out an engagement ring and two wedding rings. I thought we could try to get matching wedding rings he added. I began to feel very excited and gave Rupert and hug and a kiss. 'Let's go,' he said, 'I asked for my car to be brought here this morning, so we can go where we want.

Of course, it wasn't just any old car, it was a sports car. He opened the passenger door and helped me to settle in and quickly came round to the drivers' side. And off we went!

We were heading towards Oldnewtown, passing the Plodders Farm and further on, past Heavenly Blooms. 'We will go in there on our way back,' Rupert said, you will be able to order your wedding flowers there.' I told him how I had wished to visit it on my day off and was really looking forward to going there today. Finally, we reached Oldnewtown centre and parked outside a Jewellers, Bling, Bling and Moore Bling. Getting out of the car we walked to the door which gave a loud ringing sound as we entered. A rather old gentleman approached, asking how he could help us. Rupert replied we would like to look at engagement rings and wedding rings. What is your favourite stone Rupert asked me, and after a little thought I decided a plain diamond would do. 'OK Diamond it is,' he said, 'a single stone or two or three more.?' Turning to the old gentlemen, Rupert asked him to bring a tray of diamond rings. Leaning forward the old gent whispered, 'What price range Sir?' Rupert responded by saying anything up to two thousand pounds please. 'Very well Sir.'

Meanwhile I was looking at matching ring sets and fell in love with a pair that had a white gold band in the middle of two gold bands. I turned to look towards Rupert and motioned for him to come closer. I showed him the ones I really liked, and without even looking at the price, he took them over to the counter where the old man was placing several pads of engagement rings. He told the man we would like these wedding rings in our sizes and invited me to find an engagement ring that complimented the wedding ring I had chosen. This took quite a while, but between us we found one that was perfect. It had a gold band, but the diamond had a white gold mount. They looked good together. Rupert asked me to try the ring on, as it might need resizing. Fortunately, it was the perfect fit. (*Well, this is a story and as the writer, I am allowed to make things too good to be true!*) Holding my hand, Rupert placed a kiss on it and turning to the man, saying, 'You are one of the Mr Blings I guess, we would like these wedding rings in our sizes please and we would appreciate them being available as soon as possible.' 'Yes Sir,' Mr Bling replied, let me take both ring sizes and I will see if we have them in stock. If not, we can get them on order to be delivered within two days. How would you like to pay?' Rupert took out his bank card in readiness while our ring fingers were measured. Picking up an old phone, Mr Bling rang through to a back room and asked whoever answered to check if the rings in our size were in stock. A few minutes later the phone rang, Mr Bling picked it up and said, 'yes Annie.' We could hear her talking but not what she said.

'Putting the phone back on its rest, turned to us and confirmed the rings were in stock.

A small door in the wall suddenly opened, which made us both jump, and two ring boxes were pushed through. Mr Bling picked them up and placed them on the counter. 'Do feel free to try these on,' he said. Rupert and I did so, smiling when they were a perfect fit. After Rupert paid for the rings, put them in his pocket, and we left. 'Just time for a bit of lunch,' he said, 'Shall we find a nice café?' I told him about Forget-me-not Tea Rooms and leaving the car where it was, we wandered along the road to the tearoom. We entered and found a table near a window. Aunty Aspicity came to take our order, smiling as she remembered me from my last visit. 'Hello again,' she said, 'what would you like today?' I looked at Rupert who was looking at the menu. I would like a baked potato with cheese please and a pot of tea, and a piece of cake too. I decided to join him, but I asked for coleslaw with my potato.

Chapter 40

With lunch finished and paid for, we went back to the car. Rupert took a ring box out of his pocket and taking hold of my left hand and saying, 'Let's make this official,' slid the ring on the third finger. He leant in for a kiss, which left me feeling rather hot and flustered. 'Now on to Heavenly Blooms so you can decide what flowers you would like in your bouquet. I was close to melting into a puddle of happiness.

After parking the car, we headed into Heavenly Blooms and were met by Dolly Daydreams herself. 'Welcome,' she said, 'You must be the happy couple I am waiting for. Rupert explained he had phoned to say we would be coming. Dolly pointed to a pretty little shed with comfortable looking chairs, books and magazines. 'In you go,' she told Rupert, 'You are not allowed to see the flowers until your wedding day.' And in he went, chose a magazine and sat down in one of the comfortable chairs. He blew me a kiss and Dolly led me away to the cold room where all the flowers are kept.

Such awas a dazzling display of every flower imaginable, almost an overload of nature's beauty. Dolly asked what flowers I would like, and I asked for Freesias, Lily of the Valley, Forget-me-nots and small yellow roses with a bit of Gypsophila, if at all possible, but I know it might be difficult to have them all. I would like a small hand-held bouquet please. Dolly went to a desk in the corner and brought a picture of a bouquet similar to the one I had asked for so I could confirm it was what I wanted. Dolly said it might be difficult to get Lily of the Valley, but would I be happy with a few artificial ones? She took me to an area that had artificial flowers and showed me the Lily of the Valley ones, they were almost perfect, so, of course, I agreed.

Dolly went to her desk and started to write down a list of the flowers and their prices. The final amount was a lot less than I was expecting, so I asked her if she would like to decorate the chapel too and stay for the wedding. Dolly instantly agreed, saying nobody had asked her to do that before. I told her it wasn't that big and asked her to estimate what she would need. We would need two largish arrangements by the door and little flower bunches on the end of the pews, twenty at the most. I would leave it up to her what she did. Ater a few minutes, when Dolly was working out the cost in her head, she added the two totals together and I paid using my Bank Card.

We returned to the shed where Rupert was waiting. 'All done?' he asked, 'How much do I owe you?' 'Yes, all sorted.' I replied, 'I have paid myself, as I shall for my wedding dress.' Dolly asked me to give her a few days' notice of the wedding date to enable her to get everything sorted. We thanked her again and left.

'Now,' Rupert said, time to go check out the house.' On the way I told him about the beautiful flowers in the cold store and that I had asked Dolly to do flowers for the church too and invited her to the wedding. Rupert laughed, and said the wedding was getting bigger by the hour. 'Here we are,' he said, pulling up in front of an interesting house. It was painted white, had a central front door, with a small open porch, window boxes and hanging baskets in full bloom. Although I had seen the photo on the Estate Agents leaflet, it looked even nicer. We got out of the car, and although we should have waited for the Estate Agent to arrive, Rupert opened the gate and we walked up the path to the front door, which opened before we had a chance to knock. 'Come in, come in,' said the elderly man, 'come wait inside for the estate Agent.' He took us to the kitchen and offered a cup of tea, which we gratefully accepted. He introduced himself as Hans Kneesan. He asked our names and asked us to sit ourselves down at the table. He told us he was only selling the house because he had lost his wife of forty three years a year ago and he was feeling lonely as he had no relatives in this country. He was from the Netherlands and he was going back as he had family there. We were both expressing our sympathy when the Estate Agent arrived. He wished us a Good Afternoon and introduced himself as John Honest from Honest, Truley and Mountbatten, adding that he saw we had all met and suggested we got on with the viewing.

We both stood up, finding him a bit abrupt, but followed him into the lounge, which was a nice sized room in the front of the house. Across the hall was a room of the same proportions, being used as a dining room. We were then taken upstairs and shown the three bedrooms and a modern bathroom. Back down downstairs we followed him, and into the kitchen. He then pointed to a conservatory on the back of the house with doors opening to the garden. We followed him into the garden, finding a patio with garden furniture and he led us to the left and pointed to a garden pond with fish in. He turned round to us tripped and fell straight into the pond. We watched in horror as the weight of his body falling in sent water rushing over the edge, luckily with no fish, reaching us on the patio. We were frozen for a few seconds and only moved when a spluttering John Honest rose to his feet, water pouring off him back into the pool, his glasses askew, with weed in his hair and on his shoulder. His clipboard was also the worse for wear and was floating merrily on the water.

We all moved forward at once to help him out of the pond. He had a small cut on his forehead. Rupert helped him out, straightened his glasses, removed the weed from his hair and shoulder, and retrieved his clipboard.

Hans looked mortified and went indoors to get a towel, while Rupert, who was grimly trying not to laugh.

Rupert suggested Mr Honest go home and get a change of clothing, assuring him we would contact him to let him know our decision about the house. Mr Kneesan offered him the towel and when he had dried himself off a bit, took him round to the side gate to his car.

 By now both Rupert and I were leaning against each other in fits of laughter, with Mr Kneeson joining in on his return.

Sitting on the patio a while later, we offered a price that was accepted by Mr Kneeson, who had asked us to call him Hans. Of course, we were going to buy his house, we had totally fallen in love with it. We already had a memory, that of the Estate Agent falling into the pond. We took another tour of the house and garden, making a few notes, then thanking Hans, made a move towards the front door. We shook Hans hand (*say that when you've had a few*) and invited him to our wedding if he was still in the UK, although the date was yet to be set, but it would be soon. We drove back to the Base in very happy frames of mind. Everything seemed to be coming together well.

When we got back to our room Rupert phoned John at the Estate Agents and confirmed the price for the house that had been accepted by Mr Kneesan. He asked that they move as quickly as they could towards our purchase. He also apologised to him for laughing when he fell in the pond. Mr Honest replied that he could see the funny side of it himself now, and also apologised for his attitude to us when he first arrived at the house. That evening we went out for a meal to privately celebrate our engagement and the purchase of a house, returning to the Base just after eleven. A car had been arranged to take me back home the next day after lunch.

In the morning Rupert took me to meet the Chaplain and show me the small chapel, where we could be married if I wished. The Chaplain, Reverend John Thomas, was a plump, happy looking man and, although the chapel was small, when it was full of flower arrangements, it would look very pretty. I agreed it would be a wonderful place to be wed and we booked our wedding for two weeks' time by Special Licence, which the Reverend would help Rupert with. We chose two hymns, Morning has Broken and I Vow to Thee my Country, as a homage to the Airforce and because I had always loved it. The Chapel was able to hold twenty people comfortably, so our invitations had to be kept below that number. It was my job to write the invitations as soon as I could and get them in the post.

Our list included -

Air Vice Marshal Topman-Gallant

Wing Commander Johnny Kamikarzy

Wing commander Betty Bouncers

Flying Officer Skip Roper-Skipson

Ginny Vagaries

Clara Carbunkle

Hans Kneesan

Dolly Daydream

Goldie Gobbogogger

Sally Serene

Angie Reddit

Paula Lawlar

Barbara Bloomers

Peri Summerbottom

Plus some of Rupert's friends I hadn't met yet

Airman Billy (Bobcat) Boreman

Airman Josh (Jonty) Tyrone

Airman Sherman (Tank) Herman

Airman Todd (Toddle) Traipster

Mrs Ivy Creeper (Rupert's Mother's Sister's Husband's Daughter (Old School Friend)

Mr Rob Robinson (Teacher who took Rupert under his wing and encouraged him to apply to join the Airforce.

We were not going on a Honeymoon straight away but would book somewhere later in the year. We had so much to do regarding the house, A bit of decorating, buying furniture, kitchen equipment, almost everything will be new.

Rupert would be taking on his new position and needed time to settle into it and find his feet. When we moved into the house, we were going to get a dog. Probably a rescue, but on the large side, so I would feel safe if and when Rupert had to travel abroad. It was part of his job to attend conferences and update training, which could be held in places like America or even China. I was also pleased I had friends in the Base, so I would be able to socialise safely.

We ordered food to be brought to our room. We both felt sad that I would be leaving the next day, but there was so much to be done at home. I had a long list of items to purchase, most of which I would have delivered to the Base to be put into storage until we moved into the house. I had no idea how much stuff was needed just in the kitchen, let alone the bathroom and bedrooms. Another list was called for, and we listed most things while we ate dinner. Rupert left it up to me what makes and types and designs I bought. 'After all,' he said, 'it's a pink job!'

Of course, my first job was the invitations. Speak to Dolly to let her know she would be able to go and see the Chapel, she would just need to phone Rupert and he would arrange it.

Another goodbye, after a kiss and hug, I got into the car that would be taking me home. Zac was driving again, so at least he knew where he was going. I concentrated of one of my lists, thank goodness for online shopping. First room was the kitchen and I made good headway with that. Saucepan sets, a wok, cutlery, a 20-piece crockery set, service utensils, an Air Fryer. Slow Cooker. A good start I felt, and all being sent to the Base.

We arrived at Clara's and she invited Zac to come in for a bit of refreshment and a rest before returning to the Base. He agreed, which surprised me, but I went upstairs to my room to drop my overnight bag and take off my coat and shoes and slip on some slippers. Going back downstairs, I found both sitting at the table with a cup of tea and a piece of cake. Clara poured me a cup and pushed the cake towards me. I cut a slice and just sat back leaving them to chat away like old friends. It did cross my mind that perhaps another romance could be in cards, but I left them to it and went inside my head, reliving the last couple of days.

'Oh,' said Clara, let me 'look at your ring. isn't it beautiful!' She took my left hand and told me how lovely it was, some people go for large stones that just look wrong on their finger, but you have chosen one the perfect size. I told I knew as soon as I saw this one it was what I wanted. We also have matching wedding rings; things are moving so quickly.

I took a sip of my tea and told her we had found the perfect house and were hoping the purchase would go ahead quickly. I added that we had set a date and I had so much to do in the two weeks before. It was to be held in the small Chapel on the Base at 3.30pm two Saturdays from then. Everyone was to congregate in the Naafi and would walk to the Chapel from there.

Zac, after congratulating me, got up to go. He thanked Clara for the tea and said he would probably be the driver who would be picking up Clara and my friend Ginny for our wedding. Clara saw him to the door and came back with a big smile on her face, saying, 'Such a lovely man.' 'He certainly seems so.' I replied.

Chapter 41

The next few days just flew by. Clara's friend arrived and she showed her over my house. They came back to say her friend loved it and the area and would be approaching the Estate Agents with an offer. I found this offer acceptable and accepted. I explained the situation to her about me having to move quickly and as she was a cash buyer she agreed to moving quickly on her purchase. She had already sold her own property and was living in a hotel until she had found somewhere suitable. (*No, I know in real life things don't slot into place like this either, but I am going with the flow as the folks in this book seem to have taken on a life of their own.*)

Because my house sale went through quickly, I packed up all my goods and chattels and moved into an hotel close to the Base the day before we married.

Rupert and friends had a Stag Night at The Bopping, while my Hen Night was held in the hotel where I was staying. They closed off a corner of the bar for us and piped in some disco music. Several friends were also staying at the same hotel, so we made up quite a party with all age groups dancing and singing together. I was taking a break for a few minutes and sat watching my friends. I couldn't help thinking how lucky I was. My friends were all so happy for me and close ones had given me personal gifts. Clara gave me a little teddy bear with forever friend on it. Dolly gave me a framed picture of Forget-me-nots and Freesias laying on a table next to a wedding veil and had our names and the date of our wedding written on the frame. Goldie had taken a copy of our wedding reception menu which showed our names and wedding date which she had placed in a special folder in the front of a photo album.

I had asked Ginny to be my flower girl a few days before. Ginny had agreed and I contacted Dolly to make her a small hand tied bouquet with one flower each the same as in my bouquet. Bless her Dolly said she would be happy to do that at no extra charge. Before we went down for the Hen Party, I had given Ginny a 'Best Friend' bracelet in thanks and because she was. Ginny had also given me a gift. It was a silver ring with a rose quartz crystal in it, rose quartz meaning love. Looking at it, I could feel my eyes misting over, but before the tears could fall, Ginny came and pulled me to my feet to dance to the song 'Celebration.'

It was midnight and with multiple hugs and 'see you soons' we headed to our rooms. Ginny's room was next to mine, and she came in with me so we could chat for a while. We ordered two drinking chocolates to be delivered to my room and we sat cross-legged on my bed reminiscing over our long friendship. How we had learned to roller skate together, then to ride a bike. The adventures we went on with a sandwich and drink in our saddlebags, cycling to a pond five miles away. We would eat our sandwiches straight away and pool our pocket money together to buy a fishing net to catch tiddlers, which we would put into a jar filled with pond water. When we were bored with that, we would pour them back into the pond and hide the jar in the bushes for the next time.

We moved on to our early teenage years when we developed spots and hated the girls who didn't.

Then on to college where we fell in love with the same young man from afar and didn't talk for two days. It was only when he walked by us one day and we heard him speak in a squeaky voice, did we know our hero had feet of clay.

And now, here we were, the night before my wedding and realising things were changing but promising to message each other as often as we could.

I yawned and Ginny took it as a signal to leave, gave me a hug and left. I got up to put the tray with the empty cups outside the door to be collected and locked it. I got undressed, removed my makeup, put on moisturiser and fell into bed.

Chapter 42

Our Wedding Day

I awoke to the sound of birdsong and lay there anticipating the day. Oh, how I wished my parents were alive to see this day, but comforted myself with the knowledge that soon I would have Rupert to share my life with, I would no longer be alone.

Eventually I got up and went into the bathroom to take a shower and wash my hair. I made myself a cup of tea, nibbled on a biscuit, and watched television for half an hour or so. I knew Ginny, Barbara and Dolly were coming in under an hour to help me get ready, so I decided to just relax and try to stop my brain going into overload.

My thoughts went to my Mum and Dad and how I wished they were here. I got my bag and took out my mobile phone. I opened the cover and from one of the slots, I withdrew a photo of them. 'Well Mum and Dad, 'I said, 'today I am marrying the loveliest man I have ever met. I know you would love him, and he would love you too. I could feel tears filling my eyes, and quickly wiped them away as I heard my friends chattering outside the door. I ran to open it and in they burst.

'So here we are,' Ginny said, 'all ready to turn the ugly duckling into a beautiful swan. We all laughed, and Ginny grinned saying, 'But first things first, let's get some brunch first. It's a long time until your Wedding Breakfast and we don't want you fainting at the altar with hunger. So saying, she phoned down to the desk to ask for suitable finger food for four to be delivered to my room, together with Pots of tea and coffee, with milk, cream and sugar. While we waited for the food to arrive, they started to unpack their tools of the trade in readiness for my makeover!

Ginny cleared off the coffee table in the corner of my room in readiness for the food, which arrived ten minutes later. There were small egg and cress rolls, pigs in blankets, chips in a metal container with a paper doily, dips with celery, carrot and bread sticks, scotch eggs halved, toast with butter and the choice of sweet or savoury spreads, bite sized cheese scones and the tea and coffee in tall flasks, milk and sugar. Plates and serviettes. We let Barbara and Dolly sit in the chairs by the table and sat on the edge of the bed. I just realised I could smell Freesias and looked towards Dolly asking, 'are those for my hair?' As she had just taken a bit of an egg and cress roll, she could only nod.

When we had finished, we loaded our plates and cups onto the trolley with the serving plates and flasks and left it outside the door to be collected by the staff later. Barbara produced a bottle of champagne and four plastic wine glasses and poured a generous amount in each and gave us all one. I went in to clean my teeth again and dampen down my hair in readiness for Barbara to trim my hair and then blow dry it. When she was finished, Ginny opened her makeup kit and began to transform me into a princess. At least, she said she was, and I couldn't argue because I was not allowed to look in a mirror.

By now time was getting on and Dolly and Barbara left to get changed ready for the wedding. Ginny stayed with me and changed into her outfit there to make sure I didn't take a cheeky peep.

She put on her own makeup and slipped into her dress that she had put in the wardrobe the night before. She looked stunning in a floaty pale yellow flowery maxi dressed, which she wore with flat white sandals and a white hat with yellow daises clustered on one side of the brim. She produced a yellow handbag and a white shawl or later in the evening. She was perfect to be my flower girl.

With another quick rap on the door Barbara and Dolly re-entered, bringing Clara with them. Barbara looked lovely in a summery lavender two-piece suit, with white high healed sandals and wearing a lilac Fascinator. Dolly was wearing a turquoise dress with a flowing white ankle length lacy cardigan, with turquoise shoes and handbag. She was carrying a box and I could see the top of my bouquet and Ginny's handtied matching flowered bouquet, which she placed on the bed. I wondered why Clara was there but was very pleased to see her.

Clara was dressed in navy and white, with matching accessories and small hat with feathers that trembled every time she moved her head. (I was surprised she wasn't wearing purple though.)

Clara hugged me saying, 'I hope you don't mind, but I am here as your stand in Mother. I have known you or many years and I am very, very fond of you. I asked Ginny if she thought it would be ok or me to do this and she agreed knowing you would be missing your parents. I as so happy to agree. She kissed me on both cheeks and turning to the others asked them to take the cover off my wedding dress and help her lift it over my head. They quickly complied and as the cover came off, gave gasps of pleasure. I had chosen a cream wedding dress overlaid with the palest yellow fine lace. It had long lacy sleeves, a yellow band around my waist and a scalloped edge. Clara instructed me to lift my arms and between them they lifted the dress over my head and sighed as it settled down over my hips to the floor. Clara zipped up the back of it. I put my feet into white satin pumps. Clara then straightened the dress, fussing unnecessarily, and I saw she had tears in her eyes. She told us she had never been lucky enough to have a daughter, but being allowed to take my mother's place was the next best thing. She then held out a blue garter to be my something blue, which I slipped on straight away. I had borrowed a pretty hanky with lily of the valley embroidered on it from Dolly and I had loaned my Dad's watch to Rupert to wear on his waistcoat. By now, all of us were snivelling, and Ginny quickly passed around the tissues. I gave Clara a hug and thanked her for her thoughtfulness.

After we had all wiped our eyes and blown our noses, Dolly asked me to sit on the stool facing away from the mirror. Doing as I as told, I sat watching her remove a circlet headdress with a veil made of the same lace as covered my dress. Into the circlet she had woven gysophila, yellow freesias, small, yellow roses and artificial Lily of the Valley. She placed this on my head with the veil hanging down the back. She clipped it in place with kirby grips that could not be seen. She then lifted the veil and placed one piece over my head, leaving another hanging down my back. She asked me to stand and turn around.

Ginny had borrowed a dressing room mirror which was now placed close to the window. She and Clara led me to stand in front of it. 'Is this me?' I asked. I felt like the most beautiful woman in the world. Ginny stepped forward and lifted the veil back off my face, so it again hung down the back. 'Yes,' she said, 'this is definitely you'. I stared at my reflection for a while, then turned to thank all my dear friends for everything they had done.

It was time for us to go to the Base. The receptionist phoned up to say the cars had arrived, so Dolly quickly handed me my bouquet and Ginny her flowers., giving us both instructions on how to hold them. When I looked down at my flowers, I saw there was a glass open faced locket with a photo of my Mum and Dad in it. I teared up again as Dolly told me Rupert had had it made for me, so I would feel they were there. She added that Ginny had supplied the photo. Ginny said she hoped I wouldn't mind but she had cut their heads out of a larger photo. Wordlessly, I shook my head inferring that I didn't mind at all.

We all gathered our things and headed towards the lift. I felt like a queen as I stately walked along and luckily two lifts came together so Clara and I got into one and the others in the other. We arrived together at the ground floor and as the lift door opened and round of applause and calls of good luck were called from staff and other visitors. Thanking them all, we headed out of the double front doors to see two shiny black limousines with large white ribbon bows on the front. Ginny was supposed to travel with me, but I asked her if she would mind if I asked Clara to as I wanted to ask her to walk me down the aisle. Ginny said that was such a good idea and happily directed Clara to go with me. The other car drove off and Clara and I settled into ours. As our driver began to drive away, I turned to Clara and asked her if she would please walk me down the aisle. I was going to go on my own, but I would be honoured if she would be my stand in Mum again. Clara nodded her head, and both of us smiling at each through tears.

Before long we were driving through the gates to the Base. Ginny was waiting for us outside the door of the room I was staying in, with the door open. The driver assisted me from the limo and Ginny came forward to take my hand. He then went round to help Clara, who walked towards us, and we all entered the room together. Ginny explained we had to wait for at least ten minutes while the guests were led from the Naafi to the Chapel. We could hear the buzz of voices and stood at the window watching the guests entering the Chapel. I began to feel excitedly nervous. Clara came and held my hand one side and Ginny took the other, assuring me all was well. We looked towards the chapel again and Rupert's best man put his thumb and first finger to his lips and whistled loudly.

That's our signal, Ginny said. She handed me my bouquet and picked up her flowers. Hang on, she said, pulling a yellow rose from her bouquet and taking a pin out of an emergency sewing set in her bag, fixed it to Clara's dress. 'There,' she said,' Now you really look the part.

With Clara holding my hand, and Ginny   following behind, we walked towards the door of the chapel. I stopped to admire the flower arrangements on either side of the door and, lifting up my skirt, entered the chapel.

There was Rupert waiting for me, when the music started to play, he turned and smiled at me.

With Clara and Ginny in support, I walked towards my future!

Epilogue

After our wedding we celebrated with our friends and dance the night away. At around 10.30pm Clara and Ginny helped me change into going away clothes.

I thought we would be going straight to the house without a honeymoon, but Rupert had Booked us into a Shepherds Hut for five days. It was situated on a farm about half an hour's drive away and was surrounded by fields and trees, with a view to die for. Beside the hut was an open-air hot tub, a toilet and shower and a log burner with a supply of logs. There was also a covered patio with two sun loungers. We slept inside in a comfortable bed one end of the room with a small kitchen and seating area.

We moved into Happy Ours, which was what we decided to call our house. We didn't make too many changes, but we did fill in the pond for obvious reasons.

Clara and her friend came to visit us once a month or so. She and Zac became good friends (*I do not know how good.*)

Ginny met someone at our Reception and became

away to carry out special duties, she comes to stay with me or a few days.

Barbara was given promotion and moved to another base. We message each other often.

I have taken on a part time job doing the books or local businesses. However, I am expecting our first child in six months, so I will have to see if I can work around care for the new baby.

I see Dolly at least once a week, as I do the books For Heavenly Blooms.

The Wing Commanders continue working on the Top-Secret projects together; they are almost like an old married couple. Last heard, they were in Iceland, trialling the Stealth Drone.

Goldie and Ben are still together.

I have NOT been riding again.

But we do have a dog – it's not a big one, I fell in love with a Miniature Wirehaired Dachshund, who we named Trudi. She maybe small, but she has a big heart.

I hope you have enjoyed this book. It has not followed the path I thought it would, but the characters seemed to come to life and carried the story forward.

I have people to thank of course.

My husband Bill for the numerous cups of tea he made me.

For throwing mints at me ...... no, to me, when my mouth gets dry!

My friend Angie who happily read the book in stages as it was written and encouraged me to continue with it.

To our dog, Little Ted, who waited patiently for me to stop typing before demanding to be fussed.

To my Mum, from whom I inherited my love of words and who I swear whispered some of the plot in my ear from time to time.

And to you, for reading this rather odd tome.